HOW TO LIVE:

SAVING AND WASTING,

OR,

Domestic Economy Illustrated

BY THE

LIFE OF TWO FAMILIES OF OPPOSITE CHARACTER, HABITS, AND PRACTICES, IN A PLEASANT TALE OF REAL LIFE, FULL OF USEFUL LESSONS IN HOUSEKEEPING, AND HINTS HOW TO LIVE, HOW TO HAVE, HOW TO GAIN, AND HOW TO BE HAPPY; INCLUDING THE STORY

OF

A DIME A DAY.

BY SOLON ROBINSON.

New York:
FOWLER AND WELLS, PUBLISHERS,
No. 308 BROADWAY.
1860.

DAVIES AND KENT, Stereotypers,

113 Nassau Street, N. Y.

To

EVERY FRUGAL HOUSEKEEPER IN AMERICA;

TO EVERY ONE WHO LOVES NEATNESS, ORDER, ECONOMY,

GOOD FOOD WELL COOKED, AND ALL THE HOUSEHOLD

COMFORTS OF HOME,

THIS BOOK, FOR EVERY HOME, IS RESPECTFULLY

DEDICATED, BY THEIR FRIEND,

THE AUTHOR.

ADVERTISEMENT.

No man, woman or child, can read this book without being interested in its pleasant narrative and exposition of human character, and instructed in its lessons of economy, in things that pertain to every day life, in every family. It is written by one of much experience, with the sole design to do good. It is a good book, written for a good purpose, and peculiarly well adapted to the use of all new-beginners in housekeeping. It may be read with profit by all classes, and we are confident that no one can read it without being interested, amused, and instructed.

CONTENTS.

CHAPTER I.

PAGE

Economy Illustrated in a pair of shoes—Mrs. Doolittle is disgusted with the meanness of Mrs. Savery—She contrasts Mrs. Savery's kitchen with her own—How to make a corn cake—Pictures of health—Children and check aprons—Mrs. Doolittle upon corn-meal cake—Mrs. Doolittle disgusted with the economy of a supper that costs nothing—Trees that bear fruit, and trees that don't bear fruit—How to work a garden—Economy of space—The Watermelon, and where it grew—Delicate children—Going to marry a mechanic, ... 9–22

CHAPTER II.

Salinda Lovewell—A nine days' wonder—Studying economy—Economy of the bed-room arrangements—The oaken box—The lame boy, and the economy of kindness—The trunks and their contents—The economy of ventilation—Warming the house—A new radiator—The book shelves—Hanging up the dresses—Making much of little room—Economy in furniture—New use of a trunk—The Magic Chair—Mattress making—Economizing time—Making rag carpets—The Doolittle family—Fancy work—Works of fiction—The way that children should greet their mother—Lillie and Frank—Brothers and sisters—Evening readings—Good books—Punctuality—There comes father—A warm greeting—Teachings of affec-

PAGE

tion—The tea-table—Good breeding—Corn cakes—Mush—White and yellow meal—Economy of silver ware—Housekeeping—Proper food—True art of cooking—Tea-table lectures—How to boil a piece of meat—The secret of good food, ... 24–82

CHAPTER III.

The breakfast—Harmony—Economy in food—Dough-nuts—Economy of time—The musquito net—Carpets and calicoes—Grateful reminiscences—Rats and their counterparts—The magnetic power of a smile—Scripture answers—How to make bread—Saving stale bread—Bees in the city—The plain dinner—Greens—Account with the garden—Work for a day—What a remarkable boy—How he was home taught—There is a cause for everything—Studying ship-building—All for the best—Mind culture—Keeping out moths—Saving trifles—The poultry house—Deodorizing—The grape-vine—The garden—Economy of space—The cistern—Washing dishes—Something worth economy—Cheap soap—Making tea, 83–120

CHAPTER IV.

The tea—Vegetable diet—Effect of pork eating—Opinion of tobacco—Excerpta upon domestic economy—Cause of puny children—Salt, is it necessary?—Folly in eating—Digestion—Argument for drinking—Uselessness of condiments in food—Clothing—Such is fashion—Suitable clothing—Folly in eating and sleeping—Early rising—Walking exercise—Be courteous—Value of good temper—Rules of household economy—Punctuality—Household teachings—Botany—Poor economy—Economy is not parsimony—Learn to say I can't afford it—Care of the sick—Cure of Erysipelas—Family amusements, ... 122-150

CHAPTER V.

Saturday in the kitchen—The rice pudding—Soup—Preparation for Sunday—Iced tea—A day of recreation—How to treat servants—

PAGE

Horsemanship for girls—Magnetic power of the voice—The Doolittles' turn-out—My smelling bottle, or I shall faint—Vulgar things—Forgetfulness—The visit to the country—A sensible man's will—Mrs. Whitlock—The welcome—The farm-house—Trees by the roadside — The four buildings—The barn—The wind-mill—The strawberry bed—Uncle Samuel and the children—The farm-house tea-table—Country bread—Natural homage—Meeting the Doolittles—Thinking one thing and saying another—The contrast—The Doolittle farm—Strawberries and cream at home—Something better—My dear little wife—Happy hearts, ... 153–196

CHAPTER VI.

Visit to the Doolittles—Out of tune—A garden in shocking order—The boys—Influence upon character—Rough and tumble fight of the boys, and the result—Oil upon the waters—A scene behind the scenes—Another crash—The Doolittle tea-table—The stolen milk—A lesson learned for life, ... 198–212

CHAPTER VII.

Doolittle coming home—The effect of home influences—The effect of drinking—Walls have ears—The listener—Plotting villains—Doolittle gets his picture taken—Insubordination—A family scene—Leaving home—The pledge—Doolittle in the lawyer's office—A contretemps—The budget of news—The experiment of city life ended, ... 213–235

CHAPTER VIII.

A change of character—Mr. and Mrs. Doolittle—A match broken up—The return home—Forgiveness—Mr. Doolittle and daughters—An affecting scene—Talk of moving—A death scene, 236–244

CHAPTER IX.

PAGE

Six months on time's railroad—Talk of marriage—A lesson of economy—As man and wife should live—The old house—The pleasant surprise—The old bed-room—Goodness and happiness—House furnishing—The kitchen, parlor, and bed-rooms—A pleasant meeting—Captain Peabody and Salinda—The approaching wedding day—The Doolittle girls—A great change—The way to spend winter evenings—Business punctuality—The mysterious package—Gratitude—Another suspense—The wedding and the end, 247-276

ECONOMY ILLUSTRATED.

CHAPTER I.

Economy Illustrated in a Pair of Shoes—Mrs. Doolittle is Disgusted.

"OH, dear me, Mrs. Lovewell, I am heartily tired of visiting that Mrs. Savery. What do you suppose I found her doing yesterday afternoon, when you know it was so pleasant that everybody was in the street? Oh, you need not guess; I am sure you never would think of the right thing."

"Indeed, I don't know that I could, but I have no doubt it was something useful. Practicing some of her arts of economy, I suppose."

"Economy indeed! Why, it is downright

meanness. I should be mortified to death, if I was caught at such a piece of business."

"Why, Mrs. Doolittle, you alarm me. Pray, what was she about?"

"About, indeed! Why, she was making a pair of shoes."

"Slippers, you mean, I suppose; I often do that for my husband."

"Oh, yes, worsted work; that is a very different thing. No, it was a pair of *shoes* for herself. She had taken a pair of old shoe-soles, from which the tops had been worn out, and had cut new uppers from an old pair of her husband's black lasting pantaloons. Did you ever hear the like! I was really disgusted to hear her talk about it."

"Why, what did she say."

"Why, she said, 'there now, Mrs. Doolittle, I sat down after dinner, and commenced the job, with Susan to help me rip off the old soles and bind one of the new shoes, and now you see I have got just as good a pair of shoes, and for aught I see, just as good looking as the old pair that I paid a dollar and a half for.

And that is what I call economy. Now I will go and show Susan how to make a new corn cake for tea. Don't you want to learn?'

"I told her no indeed; when I got so poor, and I put a real meaning emphasis upon the word—when I got so poor that I could not keep a cook that knew how to do her own work, I would come and learn the trade."

"Was she offended? Indeed Mrs. Doolittle, you were rather rude. You might have learned how to make a very nice cake."

"Well I must acknowledge that I did; no, she was not the least offended, but insisted that I should go down with her to the kitchen and see how it was done. I had a good mind to refuse, for I expected that I should get a grease spot on my new silk, just as like as not. I am sure I should in my kitchen; but would you believe it, hers is as clean as a new pin. Why the very floor looks as white and clean as a table. I do think she must keep that Susan of hers scrubbing all the time. For my part I don't see how she ever gets through all the work and do the washing too. I wish I could get such help."

"Mrs. Savery says it is by economy. Economy of time, as well as everything else. But about the nice corn cake?"

"Oh yes. Well I never; why it was just nothing to make. I could have made it just as well as she did."

"If you had known how."

"Why yes, to be sure; but it is nothing to learn; and then to hear her count the cost. Why she would feed a whole family for sixpence. In the first place she took a cup of Indian corn meal, not over three cents worth, she said, and white at that—I always use yellow meal—it has more taste than the white—and put it in a clean wooden bowl, and what do you think she mixed with it, to make her cake? Water; nothing but water. Yes a little pinch of salt; but that she said she could not count the cost of, it was so small; and then she mixed, and stirred, and beat the meal and water together as though she was beating eggs, until she got it into a smooth batter, that would just pour into a shallow tin pan, about an inch deep. The cake when done was about as thick as my thumb. She first put the pan into a very hot oven and let it cook until the batter got stiff, and then she opened the stove doors and set the cake up edgeways right before the glowing coals until it got a nice delicate brown crust, and then drew it back and let it bake slow a long time—half an hour or more I should think."

"And was it good?"

"Good! why I declare I never tasted anything so delicious in all my life. I wouldn't have believed it, that just meal and water could be made so good. But that is not all. Just as she had got her cake turned up before the fire, in came her two children—such pictures of health—did you ever see the like!"

"She says that is 'the economy of health.' It is cheaper to keep them healthy than sick, as well as more comfortable. You found them very neat, too."

"Neat! I never saw the like. But it's no wonder; look at the pains she takes with them. Why, it must keep Susan busy all the time."

"Then who does the work?"

"Well, I don't know. I can't understand it. I wish I could get along so. But then my children are always sick. Hers are always well and that makes the difference."

"No, the difference is in always keeping them well. But you were going to tell us something more about the cake."

"Oh, yes. When the children came in, Lillie said,"

"Oh mother, will you let me bake a sweet cake for brother Frank and me?"

"Yes, if you will run up to your room and put away your things, and get on your aprons."

"Directly down they came, and as I live, both of them with check aprons on. I should not like to see my children dressed in check aprons. It looks so common, and sort of countryfied. Then Lillie took the bowl of batter, and got a part of a teacupful of molasses, and a spoonful of ginger, and stirred it in, and then she got a cup of sour milk; and what do you think that was for?"

"I suppose to put in the cake."

"Yes, but first she mixed with it a little *super carbonate of soda*, until she set it all foaming, and then stirred it into the batter, with a little more meal to thicken it again, and poured it into an iron pan about twice as deep as the other, and clapped it right into the hot oven, where it baked until we had almost done tea, and then Susan brought it in smoking hot, and Mrs. Savery cut it up into squares, opening each piece and laying on a little lump of sweet butter, and so serving it round to each one ; and would you believe it, in a respectable family, that that was the only cake on the table. I declare I had no great opinion of corn meal sweet cake, it seemed to look so mean; and then I had already eaten hearty of the plain cake, and did not think I would touch this one, but Lillie, with her insinuating little coaxing way—I don't know who could resist her—said I must taste her cake, and with that she asked me to take my knife and lay it open, and then she took a spoonful of juice out of the quince preserves, and spread over it, and I began tasting and tasting, and would you believe it, the first I thought about what I was doing, I had cleared my plate, and Lillie was helping me to another piece; she was so delighted to see me eat it with such a relish, when I only intended to 'give it a taste, just out of compliment.'"

"Then it was good?"

"Good! I never tasted anything more delicious. I have often had a cake upon my table that I paid a dollar for that did not give half as much satisfaction; the bakers are getting to cheat so dreadfully. I could have forgiven her about her meanness—don't you think it is meanness?—in making shoes, or putting check aprons on her children, if she had not preached me one of her sermons upon economy, and actually proved to me that the supper, delicious as it was, had literally cost nothing—that is next to nothing. There was the meal three cents—the molasses and salt and soda, three cents—the tea, two cents—the sugar and milk, two cents—the butter—butter is high now, but that was not over four cents—and let me see, was that all?"

"You mentioned some quince preserves."

"Oh, yes, but she said they actually cost less than nothing. About eleven years ago—it was to commemorate the first birthday of Frank--she planted a quince bush, and then she told how she made it grow, and bear fruit. She said she always kept the ground loose and covered in the summer with straw, which she wets with soap suds and dishwater, and last year her quince tree bore more than she wanted; and so a friend of hers came and brought her own sugar, and did all the work, and put up the quinces at the halves, while Mrs. Savery was away on a visit in the country. So she proved, you see, that they really did cost nothing. I wish I could live so."

"I don't see why you could not, you have got a nice place for a garden."

"Yes, full of bushes and flowers, but I have got no quince tree."

"But you must do as Mrs Savery did; plant one."

"Yes, and I might not live till it bore fruit. And besides, I never could do as she does. We hire all our work, and I often tell Mr. Doolittle it costs more to raise a few roses and flowers than it would to buy them. But then our girls must have a garden."

"Don't you know how Mrs. Savery works hers?"

"Oh, yes: her husband is a mechanic, and knows how to work, and don't mind it, and he spades up the ground before breakfast, and then Mrs. Savery and the children, and Susan all work at it, and that is the way they make their things cost nothing. We live different, you know."

"Perhaps they make it a pleasure, instead of toil. I recollect going in there one day last summer—the door was open, and it was just at sundown, so I walked in and through the house—the tea-table was standing, just as they left it, and all hands were out in the garden as busy as bees. I recollect Lillie was saving safron, which Mrs. Savery said would sell for enough to pay for all the medicine they used in a year.

Frank was cutting his third crop of grass from the borders, which he sold to old Capt. Peabody, for I don't know how many quarts of milk. The old lady, you know, makes a living from her two cows. I declare there was not a spot in that garden that hadn't something useful growing in it. But that was not all; I do believe that garden is the great secret of health of those children.

As soon as Lillie saw me, she ran up and shook hands, and said, "she was so glad I had come, for father was just wishing that some of our friends would come in, and then he would cut the big melon."

"Melons! why, do they raise melons upon that little patch of ground?"

"Why no, I cannot say they do exactly, for the seed was planted in a barrel of earth set on the flagging, and the vines were trained up on top of a little flat roof building in the yard, and there they grew six or eight feet from the ground, some sweet delicious water-melons. That was what Mr. Savery said was the economy of space. It was 'economy of space' indeed; for underneath the barrel of earth, was one full of ashes, saved from their chamber stove, where they burn wood, and that barrel used to run off a little lye to soften the hard water of their well."

"Oh, I always buy potash."

"And she always saves it. A gallon of lye will soften a large kettle full of hard-water, and as you see, said Mr. Savery, takes up no room, and the leached ashes make excellent manure. That is what makes Frank's grass grow so rank, and our fruit trees look so thrifty."

"Well, did you eat the melon?"

"Oh yes, as soon as Lillie mentioned it, her father got up and brought it down, and Susan drew a pail of cold water and put it in; and Frank said then he would run over and ask Aunt Mary and the girls, to come and join the water-melon party; and upon my word, I do think it was the sweetest melon, and sweetest family circle I ever got into in all my life."

"And was it big enough for all of you?"

"Oh yes. I have often paid three or four shillings for one nothing like as good. And while we were eating—or rather while we were talking, after satisfying all of our appetites, Susan and all, Mr. Savery told Lillie to get her little account book, and show me, not only how she was learning to keep accounts, but how much they were indebted to the garden. Really I never could have believed it. But the best of all, said he, it teaches my children habits of industry and economy."

"Oh yes, that word *economy* always comes in."

"Well, I am sure it is a very good word, and at this time particularly necessary for all to learn, and practice too. It would save much suffering among the poor."

"Yes, it may be necessary for mechanics, and such sort of folks, to be always saving, but thank fortune, my family are able to live without working like common laborers in the garden every day. Besides, my children ain't able to do it; they are very delicate."

"Perhaps, Mrs. Doolittle, it is the garden, and check aprons, and thick shoes, and corn bread, and all that, that makes Mr. Savery's children so healthy. And certainly, when they are dressed for church, there are none that look prettier, or attract more attention by their pretty behavior; if they do work in the garden and get ruddy faces, and dirty fingers."

"Well, well, if you ain't getting to be a convert to the Saverys' economy. I shall expect to see you soon, making your own shoes."

"I don't know as to that, but I will tell you what you may see me doing—and I intend to begin to-morrow—and that is taking lessons in the art of house-keeping. You know my daughter, Salinda, is soon to be married, and I think we had better give Mrs. Savery five hundred dollars of her portion, for some lessons in the economy of house-keeping, the practice of which in time will pay it back, twice over."

"And so you are going to get her to give your daughter the finish of her education, after all you have done for her. Well, well, I am beat now."

"I shall certainly make her the offer. I have been thinking about it for some time; and now what you have told me has fully convinced me that a quarter's tuition from Mrs. Savery, will be worth more than any quarter she ever had at boarding-school, or from her music master or French teacher; for to be candid with you, Salinda is going to marry a mechanic."

"A mechanic! Oh my! the richest merchant's daughter in town, going to marry a mechanic. Well now I must go, and tell the news. What will my girls think! good bye."

"Good bye. Yes, yes, Mrs. Doolittle, tell your girls, and all the rest of your acquaintance, that Salinda Lovewell, is going to take lessons of economy of Mrs. Savery, and then marry a poor mechanic. Well, we shall see, whether that won't be good economy.

CHAPTER II.

The Merchant's Daughter—Preparation for Marriage.

SALINDA was a sensible girl, and was delighted with the project, hinted at in the close of the last chapter. She had been all her life in a boarding-school, and knew no more of keeping house, than though she had never lived inside of one. But as she had made up her mind to marry, and as her mother said, a mechanic, and as Mrs. Doolittle said, nothing but a mechanic, she began to think that she knew nothing about the very thing she should know about, and asked her mother what she was to do.

Her mother knew the theory, but as she had been a long time living in a hotel, she could not teach her the practice. She knew Mrs. Savery could, and she intended to make it an object for her to do it.

That very evening, Charley Goodman was to call and have a talk with Salinda and her father and mother, to fix upon the wedding day. Of course he wanted it soon—the sooner the better.

"Charlie, said Mr. Lovewell, I have given my consent freely to this match, but I am afraid that neither you nor Salinda, know anything about the economy of house-keeping, and if you marry a girl ignorant of that, one who has been a reputed rich merchant's daughter, I am afraid that with your salary of a thousand dollars a year, you will run under. What think you my boy?"

"Why sir, that you began with that, in exactly the same position that I am, and you got along pretty well."

"True, but I married the mother of the girl you are after: and in less extravagant times than these, and for two years she did her own work, with the assistance of a little girl she took, almost from the street."

"And so will I do my work, father, if you will give me a chance to learn how. Let me go and live one year with Mrs. Savery—I am sure Charley will wait—or even half that time. I shall know how, and I hope shall be able to take care of my own house, and live comfortably, without being dependent upon my father, or using up all the income of my husband."

"Spoken like a sensible girl, and worthy of the honest man you have chosen for a husband. I am sure he will be willing to wait for this finishing touch of your education. When will you go?"

"If you are all willing, and Mrs. Savery will take me as her pupil, I will go to-morrow morning."

"Agreed. Do you all say agreed. Very well. I will answer for Mrs. Savery. And Susan, what a proud day for Susan, for it was her that your mother took, a poor friendless orphan, and learned how to work, and become the useful woman she is. Come wife, let us go and see Mrs. Savery, while the young couple have a chat together upon future prospects."

It was a nine days wonder with Salinda's acquaintance, and boarding-school companions, when they heard that such a rich man's daughter, had not only agreed to marry a plain mechanic, but had gone to serve a year's apprenticeship to learn house-keeping, and some of the most foolish ones, including the Doolittles, resolved to "cut her acquaintance," as they had no idea of associating with a "kitchen girl," or a "mechanic's wife." This did not disturb Salinda, as she was anxious to commence life just as her mother had done, and see if she could not help her husband as her mother did hers, to build up a fortune, by industry and frugality.

Mrs. Savery received her with open arms, and promised her, "that before a year was over, she would be just as able to take charge of her house, as her teacher; and not only learn the art of living well, but saving all, and actually growing rich upon what in most houses is wasted."

"In the first place, we will go up and see where you are to sleep. You know our house is small, and we have to economize room, but I am very much opposed to small bed-rooms, because they cannot be well ventilated, and that is of the utmost importance on account of health. I think your mother told me that you had always been accustomed to sleep on a feather bed. It will, I fear, seem hard at first, to sleep on our mattresses; but I never allow feathers in the house, except some thin pillows of old well-seasoned feathers."

"Oh, I can soon accustom myself to a hard bed. But shall I not sleep with Lillie? it would save room. I am anxious to make as little trouble as possible."

"Not much; and then it is more healthy, in warm weather, to sleep separate. This is your bed, and that is Lillie's. Both in one room, yet this thick curtain will give each the privacy of separate apartments."

"You have taken too much trouble, I fear, on my account."

"No trouble is too much when health, comfort, neatness and respectability are concerned. This curtain, being open top and bottom, will allow a free circulation of air, which will be much better than a close partition, and as we have no bath-room in the house, this arrangement will allow you both to enjoy the healthy luxury of a sponge bath of cold water in the bathing tub, every morning. I shall expect, too, that each will keep her own apartment in order; and there, see how easy it is to draw aside the curtain, and now for the use of both together, you have a large pleasant room."

"Oh, I am sure I never saw anything nicer. What a pretty toilette table; but I do not see any wash-stand."

"You shall see that. The room is small, you know, and as I expect you and Lillie to use it as a sitting room, for your work and reading, when you wish to retire from the family circle, or from visitors, I prefer to have the conveniences for washing out of sight. Look here."

Mrs. Savery stepped to the toilette table under the glass, and drew aside the snow white curtain, and there was a neat little painted wash-stand, with its white bowl and pitcher and soap dish, and drawer, and all the little conveniences. Beneath that was a square tin tub, made to fit so as to economize all the space; the whole only taking up the room of the toilette table. The stand was set on casters, and could be rolled out wherever convenient.

In a drawer was a piece of India-rubber

cloth, that could be spread over the carpet during the bathing operation. On the table was a plain square oak wood box, very neatly made, with a lock, in which all the toilet articles could be kept.

Salinda was looking at everything in silence, and Mrs. Savery began to wonder if she was contrasting it with the rosewood work of her room at the hotel. She was. And her opinion burst involuntarily from her lips.

"How much more sensible—how neat—how convenient—how good—and yet "——

Mrs. Savery furnished her the word—"economical."

"Yes, and yet how much more economical. I suppose this did not cost half the money?"

"I cannot answer that. It only cost us a little time—odd time—wasted hours with most mechanics. Mr. Savery is a carpenter, and almost everything in the house is the work of his own hands, or some of his workmen, when business was slack, or between jobs, or in some spare hour. That box is the work of a poor lame boy, whom Mr. Savery used to allow to come into the shop and make little articles which he sold in the street to help his mother, until—well, well, no matter."

"Oh yes, pray tell me, until what?"

In the mean time Salinda was examining the box, finding it was really a very excellent piece of workmanship, and "much like one of her mother's."

"Until one day my husband was passing through another street, he met a lady just coming out of a little wood-worker's shop, with that box in her hand. She knew Mr. Savery very well, and exclaimed as she saw him:

"Oh dear, I am caught in the very act. I was just going to carry this box to you as a present—a little token of remembrance from a poor boy, who through your kindness is making a good living for himself and his old mother."

"Mr. Savery was surprised; he did not know what it meant; but she took him by the arm, and led him into the shop, and there was the poor lame boy, with just as much as he could do: and he had employed two other lame boys to help him. Overhead, in comfortable apartments, lived the old lady, not only well provided for now, but her son was in a much fairer way than some whole young men of gaining wealth, and a respectable position in society.

"I am indebted to you, first, and this good lady second, for all this;" said he, as he hopped forward on his crutches to meet my husband. "You gave me the chance to learn to work, and she gave me the means."

"Oh, what a dear, good woman—how I should like to know her."

"You do—it was your mother."

"Oh, Heaven bless her. How much cause I have to love my mother. That box will be almost an idol in my eyes. It will be a prompter every morning and evening, to teach me to pray for that mother, and the spread of such a spirit as animates her heart, throughout the world."

A tear started to Mrs. Savery's eye—it was a tear of gladness, to think what a train of happy circumstances had grown out of so trifling an act of kindness as that of her husband, in permitting the poor boy to exercise his natural skill as a wood-worker in his shop, instead of abruptly driving him away "about his own business."

Mr. Savery was made quite happy in the evening, when his wife related what a pleasing influence the reminiscence had had upon the mind of their young friend.

About the time Mrs. Savery had got through showing Salinda all the rooms in the house, and that everything had its place, the porter from the hotel arrived with her trunks and bandboxes, and all the trappings that a modern lady contrives to carry with her on a journey, in defiance of all the rules of economy of dress, money, or time.

"Oh dear, where shall I put them all," she thought as she looked out upon the great barrow load; "I am sure I wish half of them were back again, and back I will send them, that is positive. I told mother I should not want them." Unconsciously, she thought aloud, and Mrs. Savery replied.

"Oh no, do not send them back, it would only serve to make your mother think you do not intend to remain long. No doubt she thought you would be more contented, if you had everything here. Besides, it will serve to teach you your first lesson in economy—economy of space—the art of making a small house and contracted rooms serve the purpose of larger ones. We are all too extravagant in house room, when it is so expensive as it is in cities."

"I thought people generally in large towns lived in too contracted space."

"Perhaps the poor do, but the fault is more in want of ventilation, than in the narrowness of the apartments. The worst economy in the world, is the neglect to provide ourselves with fresh air. In a small room, filled with human beings, the whole atmosphere becomes actually poisonous, and destructive of health, and even life, for lack of ventilation. The amount of suffering in the Black Hole of Calcutta, is a lasting memento of this fact. A great many city houses are built with bedrooms in the centre, without any means of ventilation, except through an open door into a close room, where all the cooking, eating, and breathing of a large family are in constant operation. In such rooms, human beings are expected to sleep and live. There is a great want of economy of life and health, in such buildings; but we have no 'Board of Health,' to look after such 'seeds of contagion.'"

"But Frank, you say, sleeps in that room."

"True. But look here. There is a Venetian blind window opening upon the passage, and here comes a pipe that brings fresh air from the outside of the house. In winter, it passes through the chimney, and gets warm. That opening in the ceiling is another pipe, that leads also into the chimney, high up, which gives it a draft, so that the air in this room is always pure. Now this ventilation costs but a trifle, but it saves many dollars, cost of medicine, and, perhaps, precious lives. It is true economy."

"And the other rooms, are they ventilated?"

"Every one of them in the same way."

"I have not seen any sign of the openings in any other room. How is it done?"

"You observed that work stand in your room, and spoke of the convenience of the foot-board. The air grate is underneath that."

"Another economy of space. And is that hot or cold?"

"Both. Now notice the paper border of the room. Look up and all around, and see if you can tell which of those little black stripes are openings into the ventilator?"

"By looking close, I see there are some in each corner of the room. They are admirably contrived, and I should think the air could never get very bad."

"No, not if there were twenty persons sleeping here."

"But your house is not fully warmed by hot air, is it?"

"No; because we have no furnace. We only economize the heat of the kitchen fire. When Mr. Savery built the house, he inserted a hollow cast-iron chest in the back of the chimney, where it would always take up the waste heat that usually escapes up the flue, till it is often hot fifty feet from the fire. Into the bottom of this chest, a pipe opens from out doors, and another from the top, leads the heated air to every room in the house. In the summer time the hot air is shut off, and another opening brings the air fresh and sweet from the flower garden."

"I notice a new form of stove in the sitting room."

"No, the stove is the old form of air-tight wood stoves—great economizers of fuel—and that is a new attachment, called Tillman's Radiator. You see it is a hollow drum set up endwise, just behind the stove, through which the smoke pipe passes several times up and down. At that end next the floor, the cold air, which always falls by its specific gravity to the bottom of the warm room, comes in among the hot pipes, and there absorbs nearly all the heat, which thus escapes from the top into the room, and thus by preventing the heat from escaping up the chimney, saves nearly one half the cost of producing it. I am told that where these radiators have been attached to a large and expensive coal stove in a public room, that it enabled the occupants to sit quite back, with more comfort than they used to find in close proximity with the stove."

"And not burn any more fuel?"

"Not half as much. Instead of radiator

it should be called the economizer of heat and creator of comfort."

"My mother says that comfort, health, and religion, are very closely connected."

"Your mother is right. I don't believe pure religion can dwell with squalid poverty and discomfort. The poor, miserable irreligious portion of mankind must be clothed, and fed, and better housed and cared for, before they can enjoy the holy influence of religion. It is a sad waste of time and money, to endeavor to civilize and Christianize such people by an occasional sermon. Dirt and wretchedness work no good influences upon the human mind. But dear me, how we have run off from the subject. I was going to show you how to dispose of the contents of your trunks, even in your small room."

"That trunk is full of books. I need not unpack them."

"Of all things else, your books should be in sight, where at any moment you can lay your hand upon the one of your choice. Books are great economizers of little waste bits of time. They gather them all up into a garner that will last for ever. Besides I shall be glad to have Lillie profit by your store; in it she will find something new and useful."

"Indeed she will. I have got some choice books, and she and Frank shall be most welcome. But where can I put them?"

"I have thought of that. Your mother told me that you had a good many, and asked us if you should bring them all. We said all. Mr. Savery said he would provide for them. Now see here."

She went out and brought in a set of hanging book shelves. The lower one was about three feet long, and the upper one half that length, so that when the cord was hung up on the strong iron hook in the wall and the shelves filled, it formed a pyramidal pile of books, literally "four stories" high and very neat and pretty.

Salinda was delighted. It was plenty large enough for all her books, and as she remarked when it was finished, as it hung over the work table, it took up no room.

"There now, only think of the economy of that. Mr. Savery made it entirely in an hour last evening. For your present purpose, it is just as good as though it cost forty dollars."

"It is indeed. How fast I am learning my new lessons. I will buy a yard of gauze and make a curtain to keep off the flies, still leaving all the books in sight, to tempt me, as you say, to fill up all my odd moments. I wish I knew how to hang up my dresses as well; but I don't see any room upon the wall for half I have. I suppose I have got twice too many, but it was not my fault altogether. The bureau will hold all my small things, and this cupboard the remainder; but don't you think dresses are better hung up?"

"Certainly, and I have provided for that, too, without taking up any room. This curtain you will never want to draw back any further than the foot of the bed; there, see, it draws back so far and stops, leaving it hanging between your beds. Now look again, from the iron rod that holds the curtains, I have suspended these little brass hooks by these cords, upon which, if you like, you can hang twenty dresses, and Lillie will hang hers on the other side. Then we will pin a light calico curtain over the whole, and they will be just as well protected from dust as though in your wardrobe that cost a hundred dollars."

"I declare, Mrs. Savery, I never saw your equal for making a small house answer all the purposes of a large one. Oh, if Charley Goodman knew how much I have already learned, he would think my year of schooling well paid for, if I learned nothing more. I have got new ideas — new hopes — brighter prospects. If I go on in the same way gathering really useful information, I shall make him a wife, such as he never dreamed of. I must commence hanging up my dresses at once, and to-morrow I will get some stuff and make a curtain for both sides—for Lillie and myself. She has not hung hers yet."

"No; this is a new arrangement, made to suit the necessity of the occasion. When your parents applied to us, your father did not see how it would be possible for us to accommodate you without discommoding ourselves. My husband told him that was one of the lessons he was most anxious to teach a rich man's family, how to be comfortable, and have all the necessary conveniences of life in a small house, and thus save a great deal of expensive rents. He says we are living in an extravagant period, and that economy is almost lost sight of, and hence so many disastrous failures.

There now, don't your dresses hang nice. Do you begin to see that you have plenty of room, for all your things, and nothing seems crowded. That book-case is really ornamental. Lillie will be surprised and delighted when she comes from school."

"I hope she will be as well pleased with her room-mate, as with her books and other things."

"That depends upon the disposition of both of you. I have no fears upon that point. I think the benefit may be mutual, of your associating together. There are many things that you have learned at school, and in your intercourse with polished society, that you can exchange with Lillie for what she has learned of the more practical affairs of life. Do you think you will be able to arrange all your things satisfactorily?"

"I can see a place for everything but my writing desk. I think I shall have to buy a little table to stand there by the window, just to hold that, as it will take up too much room on the work-table."

"That is all provided for. Your mother spoke about that, and when Mr. Savery comes home this evening, he will bring a broad shelf and screw it upon the window sill, which will hold your desk just as well as a table that would cost two or three dollars, while the shelf will only cost as many cents."

"And will be just as good. How easily you do teach me economy."

"That should be taught and practised in everything. One of these days I will tell you a pleasant story about a family of my acquaintance that commenced life in a log cabin, and how they got along very happily upon such a small beginning, as would frighten some of our city people."

"There now, with your assistance and advice, I am getting all my things disposed of so nicely. Now I wish that empty trunk was at home again; it will only be in the way here."

"Far from it. Did I not see in your room at the hotel, a lounge about the size of that trunk. Your mother took her seat upon it, when you asked her to take the rocking-chair, saying that she preferred the lounge. Would you like to have such a one here for her to sit upon, if she likes it, when she calls to visit you?"

"Certainly; but not so expensive. I suppose that cost thirty or forty dollars."

"And you can have just as good a one for one-tenth of that sum, and find a place for your trunk, where it won't be in your way."

"Oh, do tell me how. You are so full of contriving, and money and labor saving, that it does seem as though you could not take a step without learning me something. Do you mean to buy such a lounge as that in Lillie's room. I should be perfectly satisfied with that; it is neat and good, but still I don't exactly understand what that has to do about disposing of my trunk."

"We will exercise a little of the magic art of house-keeping, and with a wave of our wand, transform the trunk into a useful, ornamental piece of furniture. Look here."

She walked over to where the lounge was standing and lifted the cushion on to a chair, and reached down under a little border appended around the upper edge for ornament.

There was a little click like turning a key in a lock, and presto, change, the pretty lounge was transformed into an open trunk. Salinda uttered an expression of astonishment, and declared she should not be surprised to see the table turn into a big arm-chair.

"You need not; but I thought you already understood that secret. Come with me into our room."

There was a neat little round table standing in the centre of the room. At a touch it opened—one half wheeled round, and there sat Mrs. Savery in the other half, a very comfortable arm chair, with her writing table before her, with all its conveniences.

"You see how easy it is to transform furniture, and make articles serve a double purpose. This is an excellent contrivance for small rooms like ours. Mr. Savery saw one of these exhibited at some fair, and the patentee gave him permission to build one for himself. But let me show you about the trunk. You will want about four yards of this sort of furniture covering; it will cost 37½ cents a yard; and you will want as many yards of stout muslin, to make the cushions. One is made fast to the trunk and covered, and the other in shape of a large pillow to sit up against the wall, or lay down to rest upon thus. The lower part of the trunk is just covered with the cloth slightly stuffed to prevent the heads of the trunk nails from being seen, or felt. If at any time the trunk is wanted, for travelling, the whole can be taken off in five minutes. You shall cover yours with stuff to match Lillie's, and then if you should wish you can set the two together, and form a very comfortable place to lodge, or in case of slight indisposition to lounge near the window and work, or read, or sleep.

"I am surprised Mrs. Savery at your fertility of invention. But you have underrated the cost. You forgot the expense of the hair for cushions."

"No, I did not; but you are deceived, it is not hair; although it looks and feels so much like it. It is moss—generally called Spanish moss. It grows in long festoons upon all the trees of extensive forests in Mississippi, Louisiana, and other Southern States. If well prepared it is better than poor hair. There is another cheap article for cushions and mattresses lately introduced called German grass. It is a product of the sea."

"Pray tell me if your nice mattresses are all made of moss?"

"All but one, and that is the poorest in the house. We bought that as it is."

"Bought that as it is? Did you not buy them all as they are?"

"Oh no, we made them ourselves. They are better and cheaper than we could buy them. It is a very easy job to make a mattress."

"Did you ever use cotton for mattresses?"

"No; I was inclined to do so, but Mr. Savery soon convinced me that it is not a good material. It is so much of a non-conductor, that it grows hot under the body, and sometimes gets damp and musty, and of course unhealthy. Cotton packs together too closely. It is not as good either, for covering, as generally used in thick comforters, as blankets. Cotton batting after a little use gets so matted that it is almost as impervious to air, as an India rubber coat."

"What are your lower mattresses made of?"

"Some are corn husks, some straw, some German grass, and we have one made of beech leaves. I like that best of all. The material is very cheap, sweet, clean, and durable, and sufficiently elastic. Anything is better than feathers, to sleep upon."

"I don't know how you find time to make everything."

"Time is provided by the good giver of all gifts, for us all to use for our benefit, and if we only improve it as we should, we never shall know what it is to want time to do everything necessary for our comfort. I endeavor to economize time, as well as everything else, and teach my children to do the same. I never task them, so that their time drags heavy, and thus they make work a recreation. If you should ask Lillie, and Frank, and Susan, when they found time to make this carpet, they could hardly tell you."

"You don't mean to say this is home made too?"

"Not altogether. Yet it is all the product of home labor. The girls prepared the rags, and the weaver found the warp, and gave us half the piece."

Where did you get the materials?"

"By never wasting a rag. Every family could save old clothes enough in a few years, to make a rag carpet. I must acknowledge, however, in this case, that we got a great part of our stock from a friend. Mrs. Doolittle saw us at work one day and offered to give me a barrel full of old clothes, 'just fit for carpet rags.' She said she was sure she should be glad to get rid of them, though it grieved me to see such waste. There were coats that could not have cost less than $30 each, and pants, and boys' clothes, and one fine cape that had been worn by the girls, with a great spot of paint on it; and the whole so eaten by moths as to spoil them for anything but carpet rags. And then to think that every moth could have been kept away with a sixpence worth of camphor gum. And that spot of paint, if treated when fresh, with a little camphene, which is always the most convenient of anything where it is used, or with alcohol, or spirits of turpentine, could have been washed out with five minutes' labor."

"Probably it was thrown down in a pet, when the accident happened, and never looked at again."

"Yes, that is it, and so left for the moths to destroy, and finally given away for carpet rags, because the family never have any time for such work themselves."

"What do they do?"

"You shall go and see one of these days; or I will tell you, and you can afterwards see if I am correct. Mr. Doolittle was a country blacksmith, living on a little farm all his own, surrounded with country comforts. On the plea of educating the two girls, his wife persuaded him to move into town, and extend his business. He has been very successful, and has need to be, but he works like a slave, and his wife and the 'young ladies,' are ashamed to have him come to the table when they have company, because he looks so; he is not dressed as they are, who never lift a finger for any useful labor. Mrs. Doolittle keeps a cook and two chambermaids, and hires a woman to do her 'fine washing.' She is for ever in the street, or making calls, and three nights in the week at the theatre or some concert. The girls work green lions, and blue parrots, in red landscapes, in worsted work for chair bottoms that are never used; and paint odd-looking animals, among odder-looking folks who are supposed to live in remarkable houses, which the mother calls everybody to look at, as 'my daughter's first effort.' It is an effort to look at it without laughing at folly, or crying at such a waste of time."

"I declare I shall be careful never to expose any of my fancy work to such a bitter critic."

"Bitter! Is truth bitter? It is only so to those who feel guilty of such a waste of time. But it is not worse wasted than in their reading."

"Why Mrs. Savery, don't you approve of reading works of fiction—novels—or works not strictly confined to actual incidents of life?"

"Certainly I do, such books as these; but for girls like Mrs. Doolittle's daughters to read all night long such books as those written by Paul De Kock, or George Sand, or even the ghostly stories of Harrison Ainsworth, The Mysteries of Udolpho or similar things—destructive as such reading is to the body, it is still more so to the mind, and no girl can maintain her purity in such a hot-bed of moral disease. If nothing worse happens, it is more than likely, that the mind will be so corrupted by lascivious books perused in solitude that health, happiness, and life will be sacrificed upon this burning altar of Moloch."

"You make me fairly tremble at the consequences of such reading. But I am glad that you do not deprecate all works of fiction."

"By no means. The most attractive form in which history can be taught is in romance. Even religion and morals may be dressed in a garb purely fictitious, and made to serve a holy purpose. The very worst and most dangerous immoralities of our social system, may be so treated in works of a fictitious character, that the reader will learn to avoid the danger. Look at the temperance tales of T. S. Arthur, and many others: how much good they have done. But reading, like eating, or drinking, or sleeping, or labor, should never be carried to an excess. No young mind can properly digest a whole volume upon any subject, at one hasty perusal. No one should read more than an hour or two at a time. You might as well try to eat enough at once to last a week, or do a month sleeping all in one nap. Habitual novel readers get their minds so corrupted; the senses so dulled by continual overdoses, that they are only content to glance through a novel so as to get at the main incidents of the story, and the more extravagant and exciting those are, the better they are pleased with the book, which has no value in their eyes, after having been thus superficially read."

"I wish you would give me a catalogue of such books as you would recommend for a small family library."

"There come the children from school, and Lillie will furnish you with one I have already prepared for her. It might be greatly extended, but you will find in it the names of some admirable volumes that will never grow old and useless."

Lillie and Frank came bounding up stairs full of natural curiosity to see the new comer and all her things. They first gave a respectful greeting to their mother, as they always did after a day's absence, and at night they never parted from her or each other without a kiss, and never met in the morning without a pleasant recognition, sometimes expressed in their native tongue, and sometimes in French, which they were studying. From her mother, Lillie turned to Salinda and gave her hand, saying:

"Miss Lovewell, I am sincerely delighted to see you in our house, and in this room, where I hope we shall spend some pleasant and profitable hours together. I am glad to see how soon you are getting your things arranged as though you intend to be at home."

And this, thought Salinda, comes from a girl—a mere common school girl, only fifteen years old, whose manners are superior to half the boarding-school young ladies in the country. Oh, I shall love her, I know I shall. She felt as though she could clasp her to her heart, her words, her tone, and manner were all so kind.

"Indeed Lillie, I feel at home. Your mother has been so kind, and showed and helped me so much it is no wonder that I have got along so well. Indeed I shall be happy here, and as to the profit of the association, I fear I shall derive the whole of that. I must stipulate for one thing in the very outset, however. You must not call me Miss Lovewell. It is too formal. It will be more familiar—more sisterly to call me Salinda. And Frank, brother Frank, you must call me so too."

In her gushing affection she caught Frank in her arms and kissed him heartily.

If anything was lacking to tighten the cords of affection between her and the whole family, this little act completed it.

"May I call her sister," said Frank, looking up for approval of his mother, whose look, nod, or word was law with him, that he never appealed from.

"With all my heart, if she is willing, and you always act like a brother. It is the way all should live, who dwell under the same roof together."

"And I never will offend you again by the formal appellation of Miss Lovewell, while you call my brother yours also. But oh, what a sight of things, and what a pretty case of books. May I look at them?"

"Certainly, just as though they were your own—and Frank too."

"But remember, children, to use them as though they were another's, and always return them to their places. It is an act of fashionable wickedness, to borrow and keep books, and it is equally bad to misuse them."

"Oh mother, here is 'Father Brighthopes,' that cousin Josephine wrote to us about, whose character reminded her so much of uncle Ephraim. We must have it for some of our evening readings. The old man's cheerful disposition cures a whole family of the disease of ill temper, and creates happiness in every circle he enters. And here is another work by the same author, called 'Iron Thorpe,' another good preacher of peace on earth and good will to men. We will read that too. Are you fond of reading loud, Salinda, because we all take turns at our evening readings?'"

"I have never practised any, but will do my best. It belongs, I presume, to your general system of economy. All can work, or rest, and listen to the reader, and all be equally interested."

"That is not all," said Mrs. Savery, "it elicits conversation upon the topic treated of, and brings out explanation to children, of obscure passages. It is far better than any evening schools. It teaches old and young."

"And here is another valuable work. It is

Lossing's Pictorial History of the United States. Have you read it Salinda?"

"No, but I will, since you commend it so highly."

"Oh, I have learned more of our history by just looking over the pictures and reading here and there a sentence, than I could in six months' study of our old school history.

Why here is the Charter Oak, and here is Peter Stuyvesant, the old Dutch Governor of New York, who planted the pear tree, brother Frank, that you read about the other day in the New York Tribune, which has borne fruit two hundred years. And here is a block house; well, I never knew what a block house was before.

"Oh, here is a pretty little book with such a queer title—I declare we must read this to-night."

"What is it, sister Lillie?"

"Lucy's Half-crown; how she earned it and how she spent it. With some hints on the art of making people happy without money. Dear me, if it will do that, I would go around and read it to ever so many poor people that

I know. It must be a good book for children. But did you ever read the Lu Lu books? They were written on purpose for children. Ah, here is one that father will like. It is Physiology and Phrenology, by Mrs. L. N. Fowler. But the title page says it is designed for children and youth. Let us see what it says."

"Why, Lillie, are you going through the whole book-case? it is near tea-time. I expect your father every minute."

"Oh no, mother, but let me read one sentence in this book.

"We were not created to serve and please ourselves alone, while we are surrounded by friends and acquaintances."

"Love of approbation is one of the strongest motives and incentives to all our actions."

"Don't you like that, mother? I do. I think that will be an interesting book. Have you read it, Salinda?"

"Not yet. It is one I lately bought."

"Oh, here is one that we must study well. Mother, you told me about it; and that I must read it as soon as I got old enough to understand it fully."

"What is it?"

"Domestic Economy for Young Ladies at Home, by Catherine E. Beecher."

"Ah, that is one my mother said I must read, also. It is not a new work, but a very good one. Was you going to read something, Lillie?"

"Only one sentence. I think your mother had just been reading it when she decided for you to come and live with my mother. This is it:—

"'Whether rich or poor, young or old, married or single, a woman is always liable to be called to the performance of every kind of domestic duty, as well as to be placed at the head of a family; and nothing short of a practical knowledge of the details of housekeeping can ever make those duties easy, or render her competent to direct others in their performance.'"

"And very truthful it is too, and very important that both of you, girls, should treasure it up in your memory. It is the poorest economy in the world for a mother to hire a servant to sweep and clean her daughter's chamber. Sweeping is a healthy exercise, and the dust in a well-kept room is never as bad as you often encounter in the street, or on the rail road. In sweeping a carpet, some damp substance should always be used—not sand, as some recommend. Tea leaves, or bran, any kind of leaves wet and scattered over the floor will keep down the dust. Never use a broom for any other purpose, that you use upon a carpet. What have you now, Lillie?"

"It is the Elements of Character, by Mary G. Chandler."

"Ah, that is a good book. There is a very sensible chapter upon the subject of works of imagination."

"Here is a passage; one perhaps that you allude to mother. I will read a few lines:

"Let the moralist talk and write against this as he may, it will be of no use, for the mass of human minds will never take an interest in any book that does not address itself to the imagination."

"That is very true. But works of imagination are not all works of mere fiction. They may portray scenes of real life, in an imaginative form and attractive language. Do you understand? Suppose any one who knows us all very well should imagine what is our conversation and write it down, it would be a work of imagination, yet not fiction, because it would contain much truth, and a fair picture of our every-day life, and if well done, the reader would *imagine* he saw each of us, and knew something of our character. It would be a work of imagination of both writer and reader."

"Now, mother, here is a book I should like to have one like. It is the Youth's Letter Writer. You have always told me that to be able to write a good letter, was one of the best accomplishments for a child."

"Which one is that, Lillie—I have several."

"This is by Mrs. John Farrar. It appears to me as I glance over it, not only to give instructions in letter-writing, but in punctuation, syntax, &c. I shall look into that."

"I told you, Salinda," said Mrs. Savery, "that the first thing Lillie would see when she came in, would be the book-case."

"Do look here, mother; here is not only the

Complete Cook-book, but all the family. Let me see: one, two, three, four, five, six, seven, comprising cooking and all sorts of house-work, amusements and economical articles. And here is, the American Frugal Housewife, dedicated to those who are not ashamed of economy—that will suit us.

And what is this?—Oh, there comes father."

And away she bounded down stairs to tell him all the news in advance, before he sat down to tea. The others followed, Mrs. Savery remarking "that clock-work was not more regular than her husband, and that Susan's bell would ring in two minutes if they were not down in that time after he shut the front door. Every family should have regular hours for meals, and every family should be punctual. Nothing disturbs the equanimity of temper in a woman worse than waiting for people to come down to breakfast, or other meals when they have nothing in the world to hinder them. It is bad economy too, for she can do nothing while waiting, and many a good hour is lost by such inattention.

Mr. Savery was one of those warm-hearted

men that send a thrill to the heart through the honest meaning shake of the hand. He did more than that to Salinda. He looked upon her more like an elder daughter just returned from a long absence—indeed it was some six years since he had seen her—and he not only took her by the hand, but he took her in his arms and gave her a most affectionate kiss, bidding her welcome to her new home with a smile, she told her mother, "that seèmed to come from the heart, and spread over his face with a radiance of love. It is no wonder that his children love him so—who could help it?"

It is certain that Salinda, with her warm nature, could not, if she had tried, which was the furthest thing from her mind.

Strange feelings too, this embrace gave her. It was the first fond parental one she had ever received since she was a child.

Her father was a good father, and fond of this his only child, but he was one of those precise pieces of formality that never kiss a wife or grown-up daughter, for fear it might "spoil her;" or because it looked so childish to be always petting one. And Salinda would as soon have thought of putting her arms around a marble statue and kissing its cold lips, as offering such an act of affection to her father. It was this that made her feel now as though she had suddenly burst into a new existence.

"I felt," she wrote years afterwards, "as though a chain that had hitherto held me in a cold atmosphere had suddenly broke, and I bounded forward into a life of love. I knew from that moment I was a better girl, and prepared to be a wiser and a happier woman. If that chain had not been broken, I might have carried that same cold heart to my husband's arms, and never known the blessed influence of fond affection, which has been the soother of every affliction, and given me strength to perform all the duties of a wife and mother. I give credit to that first fond embrace, and its subsequent teachings, for much of my happy life's enjoyments."

Salinda was a little surprised to see Lillie take the seat opposite the tea things, instead of her mother. The latter saw what was passing in her mind and said:

"I am learning Lillie, while I am well, to do what her father would require if I was sick, or away. I shall ask you to take the same place by and by."

When all were seated, Mr. Savery said, "Are we all ready? Then let us ask Him who giveth food, to give us thankful hearts."

For a minute all were silent, and then Lillie took up the tea-pot, and offered her mother a cup of tea. Mrs. Savery replied, "To-night, at least, Salinda is a stranger—you will serve her first. That is a simple act of good breeding."

Now each member offered to another such dishes as were convenient to the offerer, until all were served.

Salinda was struck with admiration of the table furniture. Mr. Savery was a man in humble circumstances, yet the service was rich, though very plain. The sugar bowl, cream jug, spoons, and forks were all silver. The tea-pot was some cheaper, though good white metal. The crockery was all pure white, plain stone china, laid upon a clean oil-cloth. There was white and brown home-made bread, and sweet butter, baked apples sugared, cheese, and corned beef. Enough certainly, but Mrs. Savery said she would venture to say that Susan had something else to surprise them with. Lillie said, "Father you were not home to dinner, and you must be hungry."

Away she ran and brought a nice plate of cold baked beans and a slice of sweet fat pork. It is a universal Yankee dish, and a very good and economical one.

"Thank you pet," said Mr. Savery, "you know my taste exactly. But you should not offer a dish to one at table without offering to all."

All declined, but she said, "You have learned me something which I will remember."

"I told you so," said Mrs. Savery; "I never knew her to fail, if any stranger was here. What have you there Susan?"

"Only some little corn cakes for Lillie and Frank, they are so fond of them."

She set down a plate of cakes about as large around as the rim of a coffee cup, and about a quarter of an inch thick. Salinda thought them delicious; she had never seen anything like them before.

"How are they made? I am so ignorant of everything, that I shall appear to you a perfect know-nothing."

Susan was called in for an explanation.

"I mix the meal and water, with a little salt, into a well-kneaded, stiff dough, and then I take a lump in my hands and flat it down nearly as thin as this. So I go on till I get all I want laid upon my pie board"——

Mrs. Savery interrupted her with a remark that, "Susan never put dough on the table, no matter how small the batch."

"Sometimes I add a little flour as I finish kneading. Then I pass the rolling-pin over them till all are of an even thickness. Then I have my griddle hot, and lift the cakes on a broad bladed cake turner—it is like a painter's spatula—and then clap a hot lid of a bake-oven over them, taking care not to scorch them, and I don't care how hot the lid is. It is the only way that corn meal can be cooked quick. It needs more cooking than any other kind of bread-stuff. Do you think these are as good as usual? I did not think of making them until just as you were coming down. I had to hurry a little too much."

All expressed themselves pleased, and Salinda took particular notice of the directions for making, as she thought them truly delicious, and all the better that the cost was so trifling.

Frank held up his saucer to Lillie, and simply said, "If you please, sister." She understood him, and poured it full of sweet milk. Turning to Salinda she said, "Do follow Frank's example—you don't know how nice these wafers—that is what we call them—are in milk." She did follow suit, and thought she had never tasted a sweeter morsel of wholesome food in her life.

"I have eaten mush—or as Barlow calls it in his poem, hasty pudding—and milk, but I am not fond of it, for it always seems to me that it has a raw taste."

"That is because it is hasty pudding," said Susan. "Mush cannot be cooked in less than one hour, and it is better to be cooked four hours. I am very careful to stir my meal slowly into boiling water, so as to have no lumps, and keep stirring it almost as long as I can move the pudding-stick, and then let it boil as long as it will blubber up, stirring it frequently. I then set it off the hot fire and let it simmer by the hour. If we are to have mush for supper, I generally make it while the range is hot with the dinner cooking, as well to save fire, as that it is so much better."

"And still better, Susan," said Mr. Savery, "when you fry it for breakfast. But after all, the great secret in having anything good, is to have it properly cooked."

"Not altogether sir, for the best cook in the world cannot make good bread or mush of corn meal if it is badly ground. I recollect reading when I was quite a child, in Judge Buel's paper, called the Cultivator, 'that no grain but corn could be absolutely spoiled for human food, by being ground too fine,'—I believe that can; for example, it increases in goodness from corn flour, up to coarse hominy, or grains of corn hulled."

"There is another thing you believe about corn, Susan."

"What is that, sir? in the economy of its use, and wholesomeness, if sufficiently cooked?"

"Yes, and that none but pure white corn should ever be eaten by man."

"Yes, sir, I do; because it contains more starch and less oil, and always keeps sweeter. The yellow variety is best to make pigs grow fat fast. It is not so easily digested by human stomachs."

"Susan, will you tell this young lady how you keep a barrel of meal sweet through hot weather?"

"I think sir, you might tell that, for you showed me. It is very easy, though. Mr. Savery just nailed three strips of board, about two inches wide, into a triangular tube, and bored it full of small holes, and I set that up in the centre of my meal barrel, which allows the air to reach the middle of the meal, and it never gets musty."

"Somebody," said Mr. Savery, "has patented a process for keeping flour in the same way, by inserting a tin tube."

"I don't see, father," said Lillie, "how flour can spoil, when it is so perfectly dry."

"There is your error. A good barrel of flour contains from twelve to sixteen pounds of water.

All seemed astonished at this, but none doubted it, because Mr. Savery never made such a statement before his children, without good authority.

Salinda took up the silver sugar bowl to look at the mark. It was perfectly plain, but solid and strong. She wondered to herself whether their table had been set with a few extras, because she was present. Mrs. Savery was possessed with large intuitive faculties. She perceived what was in Salinda's thoughts, and replied to them just as though they were spoken.

"No, we never make any change in our table—it is the same in food and furnishing, whether strangers are present or not. We use silver, simply because it is economical; so we use it every day. In some families, it is kept for show; and so is a set of gilt china. We have nothing but what is useful, and for every day use, and we aim to have everything that is necessary and convenient. We use an oil-cloth upon the tea table, because we deem a table cloth unnecessary. We use a white cloth at breakfast and dinner, because we then have meats with gravies, which if spilled accidentally will be absorbed by the cloth, and not run off as they might from the oil-cloth and spoil somebody's dress."

"And," said Mr. Savery, "more than anything else, because we are accustomed to the sight of the white linen, and should not feel quite satisfied without it. And that is the true reason why we use many other things—habits, fashion, long-continued use, without inquiring why or wherefore, binds us in a perfect bondage. Half the women in large towns go to their meals just as a slave goes to his; because they are bid. They are not hungry, but the hour has come. They never know what they are to have upon their own table. They look upon the ordinary duties of life as beneath their notice, and therefore hire a housekeeper to do just what every woman would be more womanly if she did herself. If a mother lends her mind and hands to make her house a happy home, she will rarely find occasion to complain of husband or children seeking pleasure in improper places.

"One of the first duties of every woman, whether a mother or not, who is placed at the head of a family, should be to inform herself of the quality of provisions, and how they should be cooked, best to promote economy and health.

"An article that is very suitable for winter food, may be quite improper for summer. For instance, fat meat, or strong animal food of any kind, gives out heat to the body, while fruits on the other hand are cooling. Buckwheat cakes, which we are so fond of in cold weather, would not be at all suitable in midsummer. Again, food should be suited to the different stages of life. What would nourish an adult, would kill a babe. A hard laborer can eat fat meat and crude vegetables; but such a diet would never suit a literary person, or any one that lives much within doors. The more oxygen is taken into the lungs, the more food can the stomach digest. Every person who has the care of a family, should study Baron Liebig's Familiar Letters on Chemistry, in which he gives the relative proportion of flesh-producing and warmth-giving power of various substances, which proves the value of a variety of food. Sugar is one of the cheapest articles of human food, because it has a great deal of the oxygen-feeding property concentrated in its substance; but because of that concentration it cannot be used alone. It must be mixed with farinaceous food, or with fruits, and eaten in small quantities at a time, and then it may, in fact should be made a part of our daily diet. Crude vegetables have but very little of the life-sustaining principles in their composition, yet they are extremely valuable to distend the stomach, and mix with the meat during the progress of digestion. A man could not live upon sugar, starch, and glue, notwithstanding they contain the very substances that the chemical laboratory of the stomach extracts from the coarser articles he consumes. The stomach can create nothing. It only digests, separates, appropriates or dissolves the different portions of food received. If we are by the sea-side, or breathing dry mountain air, or the cold air of winter, we have no occasion to tickle our palates with pickles, spices, or any of the various condiments in use among the dwellers in cities, to provoke an appetite. Almost everybody eats too much. Children should never be tempted to eat more than the stomach can readily digest. Many mothers, by continually stuffing, make gluttons of their children.

"Food has been so cheap in America, that all classes have acquired a habit of over-eating, particularly meats, and the consequence is a national complaint of dyspepsia.

"The foundation of many a profligate's life has been laid by an over-indulgent mother, who incites an appetite, which must be afterwards pampered.

"Few house-keepers understand the true principles of preparing food in the best manner to promote health; and in many families, children are allowed to partake of articles daily seen upon the table, because their parents and other adults do, that are positively injurious to their infantile systems. No mother should allow articles to be placed upon her table, that experience teaches her are injurious to any member of the family. And where she lacks experience, education should furnish her the power of discrimination. I would make the act of preparing food, a part of the education of every child, male or female, but particularly the latter.

"To preserve all the nourishing qualities of meat, and still leave it digestible, is the great art of cookery.

"But, excuse me, wife, and you too, girls, I am trenching on Mrs. Savery's ground. It is for her to teach you the art of cooking. I only intended to speak of the philosophy of food, and not the details of preparation."

All expressed themselves deeply interested, and begged him to go on. Mrs. Savery remarked to Salinda, that she must expect to hear these tea-table lectures frequently.

"True," said Mr. Savery, "I have always made it a point, at this meal at least, for then we have the most leisure, that my children should always be able to say, 'I have learnt one thing more than I knew before.' I think the tea-table the most fitting place for a reunion of all the family, in the enjoyment of interchange of information. To us who labor all day, it is a delightful relaxation, and soother of our minds, after a day of toil. The tea-table is the best place for a father to discover the disposition of children, as well as a proper place to teach them politeness.

"It is a great error with all who have the charge of youth, particularly girls, that domestic economy forms no part of their studies.

"Your mother was very right, when she said that no girl was fit for a wife that did not know how to prepare all the principal dishes used in a family. It would save every one days of pain and mortification, when she was placed in a position to do her own work or direct others how to do it, if she was taught herself before that day of necessity arrived. No lady ever felt happy and comfortable in her own house, while she knew that her kitchen girl knew more than her mistress. It is the worst possible economy, thus to neglect the education of a girl, because as a woman, she cannot tell whether those in her employ are wasteful or saving. I don't believe one woman in ten knows how to perform the simple operation of boiling a piece of meat. Do you Salinda?"

"Why, yes sir, I have seen that done so often, that I should not hesitate, though I might fail in more difficult cooking."

"Tell us then how you have seen meat prepared for boiling."

"Our old cook at the school used to put her meat in a pot of cold water in the morning and let it soak, to grow tender, she said, till towards noon, and then put it on a brisk fire and keep it boiling as hard as possible till done."

"And then throw away the pot liquor?"

"Not at once. She always set it away to get cold and then took off the fat. Of course she would throw away the remainder—what else could she do with it?"

"It is just as I expected. She threw away nearly all the gelatine of the meat, and saved the fibre for food, which contained but little more sustenance than so much straw. Did you ever observe the pot liquor when it looked like jelly?"

"Yes sir, often; but I did not know but that was always boiled out of the meat."

"It cannot be boiled out; but it is almost always soaked out by just such a foolish process as you describe. Cold water dissolves the albumen of the flesh, and hot water hardens it, or rather cooks it in the substance of the meat.

"To satisfy yourself, break an egg in cold water, and let it soak as long as the cook did her meat, and then boil it and see what has become of the white. It will be dissipated through the water. Now drop an egg into boiling water, and see how quick the white coagulates, and forms a compact mass around the yolk. It is just so with a piece of beef. It contains a somewhat similar substance, that dissolves, or soaks out, in cold water, and is lost, unless for soup, and then the meat always should be put into cold water an hour or more before it is put to boil. But meat that is to be eaten, should never be soaked a minute in cold water, but should be plunged at once all over in water boiling hot. This at once coagulates the albumen, all over the surface, and prevents loss of weight or nutritive quality. It is idle to try to force the pot to boil harder as many do, because the heat of boiling water cannot be increased, and meat will cook in a temperature of 165 degrees. It only needs the full heat of boiling water until the blood and albumen is set, and then it cannot be dissolved and made to escape in the water.

"A piece of meat put down to roast, should be brought as near a hot fire as possible at first, and not suffered to heat and stew slowly. Let the outside be slightly browned as soon as possible and then you may cook slow. In fact this rule will apply to almost everything—meat, fish, bread, vegetables. Potatoes should never be put in cold water. If dropped one by one into boiling water, they will never become sodden. You heard what Susan said of those little corn cakes—she put them between two hot irons until the outside was crusted over—that should be the rule with all bread and meat, roasting, baking, or boiling, unless you want to extract the juice of the meat for soup. The great secret of the goodness of roast potatoes is, because they are put into very hot ashes or embers, that cooks the outside at once.

"There now, that will do for this evening's lecture. If too long continued, we shall tire our new pupil."

CHAPTER III.

The Saverys Breakfast.

Precisely at six o'clock the next morning, Susan's bell rung for breakfast, and in precisely five minutes afterwards, all were seated around a snow-white cloth, and a breakfast fit for an epicure. It was now the month of May, and Mr. and Mrs. Savery, and Frank, had all been out in the garden at work for an hour; Lillie would have been with them, but for Salinda and her books. It was delightful when Lillie met her parents, to see how pleasantly she said good morning mother—how do you do father—are you well brother; and to hear their kind expressions towards her and Salinda, made the latter feel as though she would not exchange her present situation for hotel life, or boarding school, upon any consideration whatever.

"Mother," said Lillie, "I shall serve you first this morning, since Salinda begs that she may not be treated as a stranger. Will you have chocolate or tea? We have discarded the use of coffee," said she, addressing herself to Salinda, "but if you are wedded to it, I presume you can have it."

"Thank you, I never take anything but black tea, not very strong, and only one cup at a meal."

"Father will have chocolate, for that is about half his breakfast."

As this meal was so much like our own ideas of proper eating, we are inclined to give some of the particulars.

The remainder of yesterday's dinner of baked beans, was "warmed over," and the pork cut in small slices, white and cold on a plate. The little pieces of corned beef had all been chopped into a fine hash, with some potatoes. All the dry bread had been made into a delicious dish of milk toast. Frank had a few radishes from his early planting, of which he was not a little proud. But what took the eye of Salinda most, was a smoking dish of grains of whole corn, as white as snow. She had never seen anything like it before. She had frequently seen what is called hominy, or samp, or hulled corn, but those dishes were unlike this, both in taste and looks. She asked, of course, for information.

"This is a regular breakfast dish with us," said Mrs. Savery. "It is both nutritious and wholèsome."

"And economical," added Mr. Savery.

"Yes, and to very many, that is the most important part of the consideration. For the last year it has not cost much more per bushel than the average price of potatoes; and it certainly contains more than double the nutriment, and not in too concentrated a form to be healthy. This is corn hulled by machinery, leaving the grain nearly whole. We often make use of another kind of hominy, made by cracking the grain more or less fine, the coarser the better, in a common mill, and then sifting and winnowing out the meal and hulls. We rather prefer this sort, and on account of a dollar going so much further in a family when expended for hominy, instead of potatoes at one or two dollars a bushel, this excellent dish ought to be more generally known."

"How is it prepared? I like the taste, and your reasons for its use so well, that I am anxious to learn the art of cooking it properly. I am sure that which I have seen heretofore, has not been prepared like this."

"Put it in soak over night in tepid water. Boil it gently in a porcelain or tinned kettle, at least two hours in the same water, adding more if necessary, and taking care not to let it scorch, and that all the water is absorbed when taken off. Keep it in the same vessel, warming it over from time to time, until consumed."

"Do you add salt or butter?"

"Never while cooking. Boil it in soft, clear water only. At the table, you may eat it with salt and butter, or sugar, or in milk, or mix it with your meat gravy. It is a good substitute for rice in a pudding. It is excellent fried in a little bacon fat, like mush, to a nice brown. We will try that some morning."

"I am sure this is a secret worth knowing

I have often thought how much is wasted in some houses, and how little is known in all, of the economy of purchasing and preparing food. I have read somewhere, that one half of the American people wasted enough to feed the other half; and that the greatest kitchen curse, was a frying pan; but I never understood why."

"It is because that meat cooked in that way, is about the worst cooked of any way it can be both for health and economy. I don't know of but one thing worse than the smell of burnt grease in the frying pan, and that is that it should be taken into the stomach for digestion. The usual practice in frying meat or anything else, is to put only enough fat in the pan to burn and blacken, and scorch the meat, or fish, often giving it a bitter taste. If any article is to be fried, fat enough to float it should be used, and that heated as hot as possible without scorching, and then plunge the meat, fish, chicken, dough, potatoes, apples, &c., all over in the hot fat at once. Fish cannot be fried fit to eat, in any other way. Meat and chicken can always be better cooked in some other way, besides frying. Fried potatoes and fried apples, if properly done, are very good food. Fried cakes, or dough-nuts, are a great Yankee dish, but are often badly cooked. They are fried in too little lard, and soaked with burnt grease, forming a most unhealthy compound. I shall endeavor to tell you by and by several methods of cooking meats, both economical and healthy. For instance, a stew that we often have and which is eaten with a good relish, is made of a pound of beef, that fried or broiled, would have looked like a very diminutive breakfast for half a dozen persons. Now, with the addition of two or three potatoes, and the gravy of our last roast, thickened with crumbs of stale bread, it makes an ample breakfast for us all."

"Yes mother," said Frank, "and the gravy on the hominy is most delicious. Besides, the meat is a great deal more tender than it would be fried."

"You are taking lessons all round," said Mr. Savery to Salinda, laughing heartily.

"And for which I am truly thankful. I shall endeavor to profit by all I hear and see.

Are you going now sir? I hope I have not detained you."

"Not long. We generally take our time to eat all our meals. I consider it about the worst waste of time to eat in a hurry. Susan, will you give me my dinner pail. I shall see you again at six. Good bye."

Lillie was not to be cheated of what she had always been accustomed to, because a stranger was present, and she ran after him into the entry, and a slight sound followed, such as has often betrayed a kiss in the dark.

"Now Salinda," said Mrs. Savery, "how have you apportioned your time for the day? for there is as much in economy of expenditure of time, as in the expenditure of money. Frank, what are you going to do?"

"I shall work an hour in the garden, before school, and then I shall 'wash my face and comb my hair,' and—you know the rest;" and away he ran to his work, whistling a merry catch to the mocking-bird that hung from his mother's window, which the bird at once took up and repeated, and so they echoed each other.

Salinda replied to the question addressed to her, that she had taken the matter into consideration, and asked Mrs. Savery for Lillie's company half an hour to go out and buy the stuff for the gauze curtain for the books; the calico curtain for the dresses, and the stuff for the lounge.

"And while you are out, you may buy some stuff for a mosquito net, which you will want by and by, and may as well have on hand. I offered to get it, but your mother would not listen to it. She said, 'I want Salinda to begin to provide everything for herself.' It is all very well. You may get your hat on at once, Lillie, as instead of half an hour, it will take a full one, and by that time you will have to get ready for school."

"And when I return," said Salinda, "I shall work till about eleven o'clock, and then I have an engagement with Susan in the kitchen."

"I wonder what is on hand?" said Lillie.

"Nothing unusual; I am only going to take my first lesson in bread-making, and learn how to do that very difficult piece of cooking, boil a potatoe."

"In buying your mosquito net," said Mrs. Savery, as they were going out, "recollect that of all colors, green is the best for the eye to rest upon as it wakes in the morning, and red or pink the worst. A light blue is very good, and a rather more durable color. White soils too easily. For the curtain, a drab ground, with a small sprig or vine would be pretty. I always select calicoes or carpets, with figures that have some meaning—something that represents something in nature. Everything of that kind ought to be made useful rather than fanciful. For instance, a carpet might be made a complete study of tropical plants, in natural colours, the names and uses of which could readily be learned by children."

Thank you, for these useful hints, particularly as to colors. not only now but for the future."

"Lillie," said Salinda as they were going down the street, "what color is your mosquito bar?"

"It was a light blue, but I believe it is among the things that were. I suppose mother will get a new one, as she says it is better to pay the expense of a net, than to be tormented a single night with one mosquito. And then, in case of a little indisposition, they are so good to keep off the flies. My father says it would be good economy for any farmer to pay for mosquito nets to enable his hired men to sleep well; they would do so much more work."

Salinda had obtained the information she wanted. She merely wanted to know that Lillie's bed was unprovided, so that she might buy two nets just alike, as well as two curtains to shield the dresses; for she already felt that she could not do enough to pay for all the useful information she was daily obtaining from every member of this family.

She said nothing of her intentions, but managed to give them all a pleasant little surprise one day, to find a net up at each bed exactly alike.

She chose for the curtain, a piece of calico, with a drab ground—like ground color, she said—with a delicate sprig of the hop in full bearing. "The very sight," said she, "may have a sort of magnetic influence, and induce sleep, as well as a hop pillow."

It was a sensible idea, for the mind certainly has a powerful influence upon the body.

It would have been no hard matter to read what was passing in the mind of Susan, when Salinda came down to the kitchen; for it was printed upon her face.

"Now," she thought, "I shall have an opportunity to pay a part of the debt of gratitude I owe this sweet girl's mother. But for her, I might have been a beggar, thief, or at best a rag picker in the street; for I was a helpless orphan, without a hand to guide, or tongue to give me a kind word. She took me from the street to a school room, and taught, and fed, and clothed me; and when she saw that I was not all viciousness, she took me home. Oh! how many poor children might be saved in the same way. But it always appeared to me that such children in the streets of a city, only held an equal rank and value with the rats. Both are looked upon as vermin that are eating into the big cheese of society, and still those whose substance they devour, only seek to punish them for having an appetite, instead of training that appetite to relish other than stolen food. Talk of economy! The worst economy on earth is this waste of human beings. Worse than waste, for these poor children are not only permitted but compelled to grow up as worthless as rats, to prey upon all that come within their reach when their teeth are grown.

"Is human labor so worthless that it should thus be wasted? What if every woman who has the means should do as Mrs. Lovewell did by me, where should we find any vagabond children in the next generation?"

It is curious to observe what magnetic power there is in a smile—one that comes from the heart. Salinda was won by the kind look and words of Susan, to feel that she was not looked upon as an intruder in the kitchen, and that she might ask questions that would tire the patience of one less willing than her present instructor, and still receive pleasant answers.

"I have come," said Salinda, "to see you make bread, and I suppose I shall ask what will seem to you a great many foolish questions."

"Which I shall answer strictly according to Scripture."

"What? answer a fool according to his folly."

"Yes, but God never intended that those answers should be such as would make him more foolish. No; if you, compared to me, are not wise in bread-making, it will give me as great pleasure to teach you as ever it did your mother to teach me.

"This is what we call a sponge. I set it this morning, and you see it is now ready to knead into loaves. This is by far the most important part of breadmaking."

"Please tell me about setting the sponge, as you call it."

"Oh, yes! Well, I use about ten quarts of flour, which I put into this large wooden tray, and make a hole in the centre and pour in about half a pint of brewer's yeast, mixed with a pint of water, milk warm. As I pour it in gradually, I stir some of the flour in with it, till it forms a batter. Then I take a handful of dry flour and sprinkle over the top. Then I spread over this a thick tow cloth, which I call my sponge cloth, and never use it for anything else but covering the bread tray. Now I set my sponge by the fire, or in the sun, and go about my work till it is ready to knead."

"How do you know when it is ready?"

"I frequently look at it, and when it seems to be working, that is, sponging up, so as to crack the covering of flour, it is then ready to form into dough."

"That is what you are going to do now."

"Yes; and therein lies the secret of good bread. Not one in ten ever kneads the dough enough. It is hard work, and requires strong hands, and can only be done by hand. I begin thus; by pouring in warm water with one hand and mixing it with the other. It will take about two quarts, so that altogether I shall use of yeast and water, about half as many pounds as I have flour. Clear soft water is the best. I use cistern water, filtered. Milk-warm or blood-warm is about right. I add a table-spoonful of fine salt. This I scatter over the sponge before I begin to knead. Mixing flour and water together will make dough, but if you want good bread, you must take both hands in this way, and work the mass into a stiff, tough dough.

"There, now, you see how it adheres together, so that I could draw it out in strands and braid a rope. Now I form it into a compact ball, and cover it up, and set it here in this warm spot of sunshine that is pouring through the window upon the kitchen table. I shall let it stand there about an hour, and then take a knife and cut it evenly into four parts, each of which I shall take separately upon my pie board, and form it into a loaf to suit one of these pans. By timing my work in this way, I cook my dinner, and bake my bread by one heat in the stove."

"What is that for?" said Salinda, as she saw her cut off a lump of dough as large as her fist and lay it aside.

"That is to leaven another baking. Do you see those pieces of stale bread which I am soaking in milk. I never waste a morsel of bread. Either in pudding, gravy, or in rusk, I use up all. These pieces I soak till so soft that I can add a little flour and knead the whole together. I also add a little shortening. This lump of dough I shall knead into the mass, and that will make the whole light. Then I mould it out like biscuit, and bake them after the bread is done, and have them warm for tea. Oh, I forgot the sweetening. I always sweeten rusk."

"How often do you bake bread?"

"Twice a week; but if I had a large brick oven I would only bake once a week; because stale bread, or more properly speaking, *ripe* bread, is for the most, healthy and economical, and as I never waste any old bread, it is no matter how much I have on hand."

"Do you ever mix potatoes with your flour?"

"I used to when potatoes were cheap. At a dollar or more a bushel, it is not good economy. I often add a little corn meal, but I always cook it partly first, in a thin mush. If added raw to the flour, it will not cook enough in the baking process. For a change, I make bread with an addition of a little sugar, or butter, or sweet lard. I forgot to say I always add butter to my rusk. Sometimes I divide my dough, and sweeten one loaf for the children. They are fond of it, and it is much more healthy than rich cake. When the writer of that text which says 'bread is the staff of life,' wrote it, he certainly referred to good bread; not such miserable bread as we find in most houses. If you have good bread, you never will be at any loss to set a very good meal, upon emergency, without meat. You may have fresh bread and butter, dry toast and butter, soft toast with water or milk, bread and milk, or, and what can be nicer, some bread and butter and honey."

"Speaking of honey, I am quite surprised to find that Mr. Savery keeps bees, here in town. I thought they must always be kept in the country."

"That is quite a mistake. Here is our garden and half a dozen others right around here, and a good many trees, and then it is only half a mile out into the orchards and fields. We have half a dozen hives now, all from one that cost six dollars, I believe, in the first place, and they have cost nothing since, except a little feeding, to save honey, and for two years we have had honey plenty in the house, and have given a good deal to friends, and sold fifty dollars' worth.

"Mrs. Savery says it is worth while to keep bees, just to learn children the value of industry, and how property can be accumulated little by little, and how we may all learn the value of improving our time while in health, to lay up a store for the winter of old age. The economy of space, too, as exhibited in the formation of their cells, and the discipline of the family to the government of one head, are all worth studying. Would you like to go and see them at work, you will just have time before dinner. I am going to set the table now."

"Oh, I am afraid to go near them, they sting so."

"Only their enemies or persons they don't like. Ours are domesticated. You may go and sit down by the hour, near the hive, and they will not touch you. Frank often goes out to play with them. They seem to know him."

"Pray let me set the table, and I will go afterwards and walk in the garden and look at the bees, and Frank's hen's nests.

"Now, don't tell me a thing, and I will see if I cannot arrange the whole quite to your satisfaction."

"Let me assure you," said Mrs. Savery, when told by Susan how she had been learning to make bread, and set the table, "let me assure you, Salinda, that while you go to work with such a cheerful disposition and such an earnest desire to learn these little arts of housekeeping, you will never find the least difficulty. It is the first great step to go at everything with a cheerful heart, and determination to do right, towards making everything right. Ah, there come the children, punctual as the clock; now, Susan, we will have our little plain dinner. What have you got? Oh! a nice piece of fresh beef, not exactly like the French bouilli, but after a way of our own. It is a piece of the rump, from 7 to 10 pounds, which was boiled in soup yesterday, of which we made our dinner without cutting the meat. It was slightly flavored with onion, parsley and thyme. Susan always adds a dry pepper pod, one of our own raising, and just salt enough to flavor it, and while it is warm she sticks in these cloves. You will find it tender and good.

"We are all fond of it cold, but if it should be preferred hot, lay it in a dish and clap it in the oven a few minutes. In the season of them, we always add tomatoes. Now we substitute tomato catsup. This asparagus you will find fresh and tender. It is a healthy vegetable at this season. How will you eat your lettuce. With sugar, as Frank is fixing his?"

"I never tasted it that way. When I have been at school, the old housekeeper was always scolding about our using so much sugar, and I don't know what she would have said, if any one had used it upon lettuce."

"She knew nothing of economy. I should have allowed you to sweeten your water, bread, milk, vegetables and meat if you liked it; so you did not eat raw sugar, you might have all you wished, that is, in place of the same cost of other food."

"I declare the lettuce is much better this

way than as it is usually fixed at the hotel, with mustard, oil, vinegar, pepper, salt, catsup, etc., and I dare say, more healthy."

"If you like vinegar, you will find the sweet and sour very pleasant mixed together. How do you like the beef?"

"It is excellent, and so is the asparagus; and these greens, what are they?"

"It is a compound, I think. Frank knows best, he gathered them. How is it, Frank?"

"Two dandelions; three turnip tops; a few sprigs of spinage, a little pig-weed, or lamb's quarter, and the balance cabbage sprouts. All good, and as I could not get a mess of either, I thought I would go in for an assortment. This part is hen fruit," said he, laughing, and pointing to the halves of hard-boiled eggs that Susan had added to the dish of greens. "Shall I help you to a little more?"

"If you please. I am fond of such food, and believe it is healthy, and I suppose, Frank, not very expensive."

"I can tell you in the fall, or rather sister Lillie can; for she sets down every day debt and credit to the garden. I wonder how much she will credit my two dandelions."

"I don't know, Frank; how much do you think they were worth?"

"Well, they were good big ones, but I guess on the whole, you may set down the whole mess of greens at two cents."

"That is a very fair estimate, my son; and I am glad to see you inclined to be just, even in your dealings with the garden. You will find it saves a great many cents in the course of the year."

"Yes, ma'am; I am going to charge you eight cents for the asparagus, two cents for the lettuce, and one cent for the radishes I shall give you for tea."

"There is thirteen cents to-day; and certainly you give us things at very low rates, and much more fresh than those we get in market. Your hen-house, too, Frank, has been very profitable to us the past year."

"And that reminds me that I must go and give the biddies some water, and cut a little grass for them, before I go to school."

"Oh, let me do that," said Salinda, "I am

going out with Susan, after dinner, to look at them."

"Will you? well, I thank you; I will do as much for you, or somebody else, it is all the same, so that we help one another, and try to do all the good we can in the world, so my mother says, and I never knew her to say anything wrong."

"And I hope I never shall know my son to say or do anything wrong."

"I hope not, mother; and therefore, if sister Lillie is ready, we will hurry off to school; and to-morrow—'Well, well,' as our minister says, 'ye know not what a day may bring forth,'—but to-morrow is Saturday."

"What do you expect to-morrow will bring forth for you, Frank, a play-day?"

"Not exactly, though I think I shall make it one of amusement. In the first place, let me see—well, in the first place, I shall get up and take a wash. Then I shall go down and help father in the garden till breakfast-time. Then I shall wash again. Cold water don't hurt me any. At breakfast I expect to eat two fresh eggs. Give the biddies credit for a dozen, Lillie; that is fifteen cents. After breakfast, I shall cut my grass for the first time. Can't tell how much that will be till old Cap'en Peabody comes with his wheelbarrow, to take it home. It will bring us milk, though, for our Sunday pudding. Then I am going to clean out my hen-house, and put every scrap of dirt in the cistern, where father mixes all sorts of stuff which makes our melons, and lima beans, and tomatoes, and celery, and other rank feeders upon manure, as father calls them; and after that I am going over to the new house where father is at work, to nail five pieces of waste boards together into a box, for a nest for my old blue hen, for she told me yesterday that she should want to commence setting about Sunday. After that, I have nothing particular on hand, and shall be at the service of my mother, or either of these my sisters, for a walk, or ride, or to work, or read, or play. Now, are you ready, Lillie? Good-bye, mother, good-bye, sister," kissing his hand to Salinda, and running off in a glee of laughter.

"Thank you, brother Frank. Remember,

then, to-morrow afternoon, you are at the service of the ladies. Good-bye. What a remarkable boy," said Salinda, to his mother, "for one of his years. I do not understand why one child should be so manly, or womanly, and another so childish."

"It is because they are kept so childishly by their parents. The mind, the natural faculties have no chance to develop their power. Infants have the organs of voice, but do not use them because the reasoning faculties have not yet taught them the meaning of words. As soon as that faculty is developed, children become great talkers, mere chatterers, many of them. Those who hear correct language, acquire and use it. Without giving a child ideas, how is it to express them? Without giving a child to understand what its ears, eyes, and hands are for, how is that child to exercise anything but the natural faculties of a child.

"To improve a child's organ of language, you must converse with that child, not in namby pamby baby talk, but as though you were conversing with a man or woman. If my children talk manly, it is because they never hear any other language from their parents. Frank may seem a little forward, sometimes, but it is because he has a natural vein of humor, and vivacity of disposition. My children are not petulant, because they never see anything of the kind at home, and the little they see abroad, only serves to make them love home quiet all the better."

"But you do not think that all children are born alike?"

"Oh, no, by no means. Some of the perceptive faculties are much stronger than others in different individuals. I have heard of a person so deficient in the organ of color, that he could not tell green from blue, or yellow from white. You seem surprised, yet reflect a moment. By candle light, you cannot do it yourself. To such a person, in daylight, the same inability to distinguish the difference in shades continues. Now it is hardly possible, if those having charge of that person in childhood, had taken constant pains to develop this organ, that it would not have been improved. Many children have the organ of Causality constantly blunted, and the intellect made dull, by that universal check—'*don't ask so many foolish questions,'*—put upon their inquiring minds. Is it foolish for a child to inquire the cause of, what is to him, a phenomenon? I remember when a child, I went with my father, who was one of those men who never could bear to hear a child ask questions, to see a fountain play. The beautiful jets of water spouted into the air, sixty feet, and fell in silver and diamond sparkling drops, all around. My first inquiry was, 'who makes it play?' I was answered quite short, 'nobody, you silly child.' 'Then,' said I, earnestly, '*what* makes it play?' I was not kindly answered with a short description of the laws that govern water, but told not to ask so many foolish questions. Do you know what I thought then? If I ever grow to be a woman, I never will tell a child not to ask so many foolish questions. Acting upon that impression, so graven upon my heart,as it was burning with desire to know the cause of that water spouting into the air, I have ever encouraged my children to ask questions. I have told them there is a *cause* for everything. Study to find out that cause. Never say I don't know, I never thought about that. I teach them to think. I make companions of them. I ask questions for them to answer. For instance: one day I saw Frank bringing some old lime into the hen yard, and I asked him what that was for. 'Because,' said he, 'the shells of eggs are principally composed of lime.' 'Who told you so?' 'No one; I read it in a book, and I said to myself, then hens must eat lime; how else could the shells be formed. I did just what you have always told me, mother. I argued from effect to cause.' This was but a trifle in itself, but it taught me what was the effect of early training upon a young mind. We have always tried to impress upon him the good effect of manly actions. We have developed his natural faculties, without crowding his education in school. I have been encouraged in this course by an elder brother, the uncle Ephraim you hear Lillie talk about. He was here some years ago, and before he started home, he wrote for his son Charles to meet him in Chicago, on a certain day, with his carriage and horses. 'Why, Ephraim,' said I, 'how old is

Charley?' 'Well, let me see,' said he, 'this is September, and he was eight in March.' 'And do you expect him to drive forty miles alone, and then, what if he should not meet you. Something might detain you.' He replied, 'The road is plain, he knows the way, and he will go to the hotel. Mr. Brown knows him, for he has been there with me. And if he didn't, the boy has a tongue, and can tell him who he is, and what he is after. He will do well enough, depend upon it, sister. That is the way I train my boys.' The result proved his theory correct. Charley went in, and drove to the hotel, ordered his horses put up, and saw that they were well taken care of, too, and he took good care of himself. My brother did not arrive for three days; the boat he went around the lakes on, having got aground, and met with several detentions."

"I should have thought Charley would have been alarmed at his father's absence, or got tired of waiting."

"Not he. He knew that his father would come when the boat did, and in the meantime he improved every minute. He studied the science of ship-building, found out how the workmen bent those great planks by the aid of steam; looked into the steam-engine shops, and found somebody that was willing to answer his questions, and teach him how the power was obtained and controlled. Then he looked into the founderies, and saw how cast-iron was formed, how machines were made, by boring, drilling, filing, polishing, and fitting the various parts together, and, in short, my brother wrote me 'it was the best three days' schooling the boy ever had. I was not at all sorry, after I had learned the result, that I was detained. In fact, I did not fret any, at the time; I knew it was all for the best, as every such thing always is, though we are not always able to see it.'

"This also taught me a lesson. It taught me that children have a natural desire to learn, and that they cannot learn unless they have a teacher. It taught me that the faculties of a child may be developed much younger than is generally supposed. We have infant schools, and all sorts of 'institutions,' to force the faculties applicable to the ordinary branches of school studies, which are pushed like plants in a hot-bed, or forcing-house, to the neglect of all the qualifications that make a man or woman of intellect.

"There, now, I think I have given you a sufficiently long lecture upon the science of mind culture."

"I think I could listen to just such a one, with profit and pleasure, every day, and I hope I shall."

"There is no telling what the next may be about. I never premeditate upon my subject. Whatever occurs at the moment, that I think I can explain, or make use of to teach those who are dependent on me for information, I seize upon as the basis of my lecture, if that is a proper term for those little conversations. You were going to the garden—I have a little work to do. I saw a moth-miller last night, and that is a warning for me to secure my furs and woolens. It costs so little time or money to pack them down in a trunk or box, with a little camphor gum, tobacco, snuff, cedar shavings, sassafras, or almost anything that gives a strong odor, except musk."

"And why not that?"

"I cannot say. I only know that muskrat furs are just as likely to be destroyed as any other."

Mrs. Savery went about her work of saving; for that is the true economy of housekeeping, saving everything—money, time, and that which cost both—gathering up little fragments—doing what most women call trifles; but, though it may seem trifling to them, it is no trifle to their husbands, in the footing up of the year's accounts.

Salinda went to fulfill her promise to Frank, to water and feed his hens. Susan went with her, and that she might not feel as though she was losing any time, Salinda was to help her wash the dishes. "But," says she, "had we not better do that first?"

"No, because Frank is very regular in his practice of feeding and watering his hens in the middle of the day; and habit with them is as strong as with us. They are looking for it."

Salinda found the same economy of space here as elsewhere. A strip five feet wide across the end of the lot was occupied by the poultry yard, poultry house, tool house, and the temple of Cloacina.

The latter bore a most striking contrast to most of these necessary appendages to every house. A barrel of plaster of Paris stood in one corner, with a little tin dipper, and it was the invariable rule of every occupant of the place, to scatter into the vault a little of the plaster, which absorbed all the ammonia, keeping the place sweet, and rendering the monthly task of emptying the contents into the compost bed, neither unpleasant nor unprofitable. That compost bed was a tight vat, occupying the room under the hen-house, and in summer received all the fertilizing liquids from the house, as well as every other scrap of waste, which not only kept the garden rich, but afforded a surplus which was readily purchased and pumped out every week, by a market gardener in the neighborhood. In the corner appropriated as a hen yard, stood a large plum tree, that never failed to bear a full crop, because the hens prevented the ravages of the curculio. Starting near the compost tank, from which the roots drew sustenance, were two grape vines; a Catawba and an Isabella, which were trained each way along the building and fence for a hundred feet; these afforded all the grapes, and many more than the family wanted, and, as Mr. Savery said, cost no room of earth or air.

Over the hen-house was the aviary; and on top of the little room used to store the tools, the lime, plaster, empty beehives, &c. &c., grew the famous water-melons. The whole of these buildings were screened from full view of the house by a row of quince, currant, gooseberry, and rose-bushes. Then came the strawberry bed, with the vines shooting through the covering of tan bark, which not only serves as the best manure, but keeps the fruit clean. All the vegetables and bushes seemed to be arranged so as to economize room, and make a little spot of ground produce a great deal of food. Next to the house was the grass-plat, and in the centre of that stood a half barrel tub, filled with earth, and planted with cucumbers. Half the vines will climb a bush, and the other half fall down upon the grass, but are not allowed to run far.

Salinda could not help thinking how much land in and around all cities is wasted—left barren and worthless, that might be made to bear rich products of human food, like this little plat. She noticed that even the earth in the cucumber tub was not allowed to remain idle while waiting for the proper time to receive the seed, and while they were vegetating, but it was made to produce a crop of early radishes. She did not know, but Mr. Savery did, that this productiveness was owing to his liquid manure, and other frequent waterings which he gave the whole ground, with a cheap hand force-pump and hose, with a rose nozzle, which Frank guided while his father worked the pump.

"I should really like to know where your cistern is. There is but one pump, and that is at the well."

"And yet it draws well or cistern water at your option. You have only to turn this cock this way, and that one this way, and now it will pump well water. Change them back again, and you draw water from the cistern, which is under the grass-plat. Last summer it got so low after being cleaned out in the spring, that we had to use ley from the ash leach, to make the well water soft enough to wash with. But after all, there is nothing like good filtered rain water for every purpose. It is great economy to build a cistern, and adds greatly to the comfort of those who have to do the housework. Speaking of the cistern reminds me that I have got some dishes to wash."

"And I am to help you—that is, I should like to learn what there is for me to learn in that branch of domestic economy, if you are willing, Susan."

"Certainly. Well, here is one thing for you to learn. Never put ivory knife-handles into warm water. I use this double tin can. This for the knives, that for the forks."

It was like two quart measures* soldered together. One had an extra bottom, that left the water just deep enough for the dinner knives, and the other for the forks, when filled

* There are cans made on purpose with bars like a gridiron, so close that the handles cannot go through, while the blades remain in the water. Susan's was more primitive and less expensive.

near the top. For the tea knives it was not so full—the can being connected, made the water always of the same relative height. "If the handles get soiled so that I cannot wipe them clean," said Susan, "I use a piece of fine sand-paper."

"Do you use soap in your dish water?"

"Seldom. That stone pot is full of ley. If I have a very greasy dish, that hot water will not clean, I dip it in that ley, and thus make the grease into soap. It is a small matter, but it saves many a sixpence in a year. When the ley gets greasy, I empty it in a tub where I keep ley, to eat up all the grease and bones that would otherwise be wasted, or get mouldy or fly-blown, if kept long enough to boil up for soap. Sometimes it makes itself into excellent soap, without one bit of trouble."

"Now, shall I wipe the plates as you wash them?"

"Not yet. I wash them in this pan, and set them in that to drain. Then I rinse them off with boiling water—so—now you may wipe them, while I wipe the knives. Now pour that water in this pan, and I will wash those larger dishes. It is not an unpleasant job, nor is it hard work to wash dishes, if rightly done; and I have not broken anything for years."

"What are you boiling the teakettle for, Susan?"

"For tea. It is so warm that I shall not want any fire in the range this afternoon—with what heat there is, that water will keep almost as hot as boiling till night. Then I take a handful of charcoal, and kindle it in this little portable furnace, and that saves a peck of coal; as the furnace will boil my water, and boil my tea, and make a bit of toast if I wish."

"Do you boil tea?"

"Black tea is very much improved by being boiled at least fifteen minutes. It changes the flavor entirely."

"I never heard of that before. And is it more economical—that is, does it take less tea to serve the family?"

"At least twenty-five per cent. That you may be convinced of the difference in flavor, strength, economy, everything, I will divide my usual measure—I always make by a uniform measure—and give one-half made in the usual way of pouring boiling water on the leaves in the pot, and the other I will boil half an hour."

The result will be known by listening to the following tea-table talk in the next chapter.

CHAPTER IV.

Something the matter with the Tea. What is it? The properties of Tea. The difference proved. Lillie's Maxims of Life.

"WHAT is the matter with your tea, Susan?" said Mr. Savery, at the first sip. "I am very fond of a good cup of black tea, and if not taken very warm, and only moderately strong, with sugar and milk, I think it not only pleasantly invigorating, but quite healthy. Liebig, I think it is, says that tea contains nutritious qualities. It is certainly strengthening and invigorating. It possesses stimulating and narcotic principles that do not agree with persons of hypochondriacal habits, or weak nerves. From 30 to 40 per cent. of tea is soluble in water. And a trifle larger proportion is soluble in alcohol. Tea contains considerable tannin; a trace of volatile oil; and the peculiar flavor is contained in a resinous substance. This is much easier dissolved in some varieties than others."

"And hence the necessity," said Mrs. Savery, "in making black tea that the infusion should stand and boil some minutes; which I perceive Susan has somehow neglected to-night."

"No, not neglected," said Salinda, "it has been purposely done, to teach me the difference. Come in, Susan, with the other. You need not stand there laughing at my ignorance, or how easy you have convinced me of my error."

"To remove old prejudices," said Susan, as she changed the tea-pot, "particularly anything relating to our accustomed food, requires strong evidence that the proposed innovation upon old customs is really an improvement. Mr. Savery, let me change your cup. And you, Salinda, will, as readily as he does, see the difference in flavor."

"And economy, too," said Mrs. Savery. "You make that quite a yearly item. This we are indebted for to Uncle Ephraim; and I remember that we all thought it was one of his odd notions, but he took the same course to convince us that Susan has you, Salinda.

We are not aware ourselves, how wedded we are to habit in our eating and drinking."

"That is true, wife. Just look at the ridicule that has been heaped upon those who advocate a vegetable diet. They have been called bran-bread philosophers—advocates of feeding workingmen upon sawdust; and a thousand other slanders; when, in fact, all they recommend is that men should act rationally in adapting the proper food to the various conditions of men. They simply say, that it is not necessary for the health of women and children, and persons of sedentary habits, to eat the same fat pork diet of a hard-working farmer. We are, as you perceive, no vegetarians, yet we must allow that the advocates of that system have a great deal of reason and common sense in their arguments. It is a pretty well settled fact in philosophy, that the consumers of swine's flesh, generation after generation, will at length come to partake in some degree of the nature of the animal whose flesh they have fed upon. Many physicians are of opinion that pork is the cause of scrofula. We cannot dispute the fact, that none but hard laborers, who are much in the open air, can consume large quantities of gross food, and maintain good health. But it is very hard to break people of long indulged in gross habits of any kind. There is not a rum-drinker, rum-maker, or rumseller, in the world, that does not know the evil effects of taking alcohol into the stomach; yet one persists in the manufacture and sale, because it affords him an easy profit, and the other continues its use, because it produces exhilaration or stupefaction; or else gives strength, or courage to do some act of desperation, of folly, or wickedness."

"You are severe on gross eaters and hard drinkers, sir; pray, what is your opinion of the use of tobacco?"

"That, waving all argument about its poisonous effects and unhealthiness, the use of it is so positively filthy, whether chewed, snuffed, or smoked, that no well-bred gentleman or lady can use it, or sanction its use, or what is still more, encourage friends to get accustomed to a practice that enslaves them through life. But come, let us adjourn to the sitting-room, and see what Lillie has to read to us—this is the end of her school week, when she furnishes us a composition, or some collation of facts gathered during the week. What have you to-night, my daughter?"

"At my mother's suggestion, I have made an excerpta of passages and sentiments from several authors upon the subject of domestic economy.'

"That probably is intended for your benefit, Salinda."

"Then I shall give my careful attention to its teachings. Will you read, Lillie. I hope your father and mother will give us running comments."

"Catharine E. Beecher says:

"In regard to the subject of health, mothers and teachers —[she might have added children]—never had the facilities afforded for gaining the knowledge they needed. It is painful, after years of toil and anxiety, to discover, that in some important respects, mistakes have been made which have entailed suffering and sorrow on ourselves and the objects of our care.

"No American woman has any occasion for feeling that hers is an humble or insignificant lot.

"Persons in poverty to-day, may rise to affluence to-morrow. Children of common laborers may rise to wealth and station, while their wealthy neighbors' children, through long enervating indulgence, sink down to the lowest station in life.

"Were it not for the supply of poverty-stricken foreigners, there would be a dearth of domestics in every family."

"That," said Mr. Savery, "is because we rear our own children to look upon all labor with contempt—that the garb of an honest workman is a disgrace. But go on."

"There is nothing that so demands system and regularity as the affairs of a housekeeper, and the want of success, through ill health and inability to attend to the duties, are causes of great anxiety and perplexity.

"Women in this country are unusually subject to disease, through delicacy of constitution.

"Curvature of the spine is a prevalent complaint with the daughters of the rich."

"Much of which is owing to their enervating habits—lounging on sofas and cushioned chairs—never going out in the air, except in a cushioned carriage—never in fact taking any exercise that stirs the blood, except perhaps a health-destroying midnight dance; and avoiding cold water as they would the plague. It is such a life that makes feeble, puny girls, and sickly mothers, who prematurely blossom, bear early, sickly fruit, wither and die. 'Tis a sad picture, but it is truly American."

"Why, Mr. Savery, your chairs are all cushioned, even those in the dining-room, which is quite unusual."

"Only cushioned in the seat. That is economy. It is not like a chair with a stuffed back, that shuts out all circulation of air from the body. These plain, hard seat cushions save much wear of clothing, and should be used at the table, of all other places, where all should sit at their ease. Go on, Lillie."

"Medical men all tell us that this constitutional debility results from mismanagement in early life.

"Mental excitement, without exercise, tends to weaken the system."

"Don't imagine," said Lillie, as she saw Salinda pick up Miss Beecher's Domestic Economy, "that I make literal quotations. I am rather sifting out facts, which I express, or try to, in short hand."

"You are very successful, and I am deeply interested."

"American women, from various causes, are exposed to a far greater amount of intellectual excitement than those of any other land, with far less walking, riding, gardening, or exposure to the open air, than falls to the lot of European women.

" American girls go from school to visiting, dressing, evening parties, balls, or amusements, in close hot rooms; morning calls and midday shopping, in ridiculously unhealthy modes of dress, and then eat gormandizing dinners, till they have to lay down exhausted, to read the last novel.

" At fifteen they marry—at thirty they are faded, worn, haggard, and discontented with all the world, to think they have lost their beauty."

" Is it any wonder," said Mr. Savery, " that such girls become mothers of puny children, or that such a large proportion of all the deaths that occur in cities are among those under ten years of age! We listen, Lillie."

" Many, in fact most, wealthy ladies would think a walk of a mile, three or four times a week, would be a killing amount of exercise.

" Girls should never be sent to school till six years old, and then the physical rather than the intellectual cultivation should be attended to. Children should frequently be sent out to play. The air in a school room should never be overheated, or suffered to get impure. Crowded rooms and salamander stoves, are the curse of American school-rooms.

" A girl from six to ten years old should be taught to do

many things about a house, so as to acquire active habits, and learn that labor in any household duty is not degrading.

"Where there are several daughters in the house, they should go by turns to the kitchen, while all the light work should be done by the others.

"Every branch of domestic economy should be taught in all female seminaries.

"Healthful exercise gives rosy cheeks, rounded form and delicate skin.

"There is no period in life when a young lady will not find a knowledge of domestic economy useful to herself and others. The mere knowledge of how to remove a grease spot, may confer happiness for the moment upon herself and some friend.

"Every girl should be trained to have some knowledge of the laws of health, and how to take care of the sick."

"She should also know how to prevent, in a great measure, her children from getting sick, by indulgence in unwholesome food. However, I won't interrupt you," said Mrs. Savery.

"Those persons who keep their bodies in a state of health by sufficient exercise, have a sure guide of what they should eat.

"Many women are so inactive, they never feel hungry; and only eat at stated times, through habit, or for pastime.

"Hence the necessity of inducing appetite by tempting viands, and a variety of high seasoned dishes. By tasting of this and that, she loads her stomach with more than a hodman could well digest.

"Health depends on quality as well as quantity of food. Some things are naturally pernicious, and some are made so by cooking and combination with others.

"Condiments, such as pepper, spice, mustard, vinegar, salt, &c., are never needed in a healthy stomach. In case of stimulants being needed, such things may be used."

"Don't you think," said Salinda, "that salt is necessary?"

"No more," said Mr. Savery, "than any of the other stimulants. If we eat less salt, we should drink less, and the world would be saved from the disgrace of drunkenness. We are so accustomed to the use of salt, that we never stop to inquire whether it is really useful or necessary, or beneficial or otherwise. But we won't stop to discuss this question now. It is enough for the present purpose that it shall induce you to think and inquire for yourself. We listen, Lillie."

"There are more gluttons than drunkards in America—that is, persons who injure themselves by eating."

"That is very true," said Mrs. Savery. "Only last month a young lady-friend of ours that had suffered for a long time with ill health, and loss of appetite, took a notion that she must have some hard clams, and in the course of the day she ate several dozen; some raw and some cooked, as people generally cook them—that is, nothing but warmed—not cooked at all—and in the evening she was taken with spasms, and came near losing her life. The stomach was paralyzed, as bad as though she had swallowed so many leaden bullets. Many a life is destroyed by imprudence in eating.

"I have a sentence that I have extracted from one of my books, just in point to your remark, mother. This is it:

"A perfectly healthy stomach can digest almost any healthful food; but when the digestive powers are weak, what is food for one, would be poison to another."

"You know Virginia had been suffering a long time with dyspepsia. Perhaps, too, she did not chew her food sufficiently, for my books tell me that 'it is indispensable that food be taken slowly and well chewed, or it will not digest. Rice, potatoes, when dry and well cooked, flour, Indian corn, tender meats, or meats minced fine, are easiest of digestion. Tough beef, fat bacon, unripe fruit, wilted vegetables, rancid butter, short pie-crust, hot short cakes, and many articles of mixed food, will in time destroy the powers of an ostrich-like stomach, in any human being that does not take violent exercise in the open air. After every meal, a person should rest a little while, to allow the gastric juice time to incorporate itself with the contents of the stomach.' "

"That is the very reason," said Mr. Savery, "why we practice sitting at the table in conversation after we have done eating. It is not time lost."

"The food of our meals should be properly apportioned to the wants of the body. At breakfast we need drinks, and should eat fruit, and light vegetable food, with but little meat. That good old-fashioned dish of hash—a little meat and potatoes, with a flour gravy, is an excellent breakfast dish. But we do not eat fruit enough, and the eating of hearty meats, often too, cooked by frying, is a national sin of this country.

"Dinner should be taken near the middle of the day, and may be a hearty one, if the proper amount of exercise has been had in the forenoon, and labor is to be performed in the afternoon. After dinner, spend an hour in conversation, reading, or light work, before you resume the regular employment of the day, and you will accomplish more before night, with less exhaustion.

"Look for an example to the sons of toil in the harvest field. Their 'nooning' is true economy.

"The true temperature for all kinds of food and drink, is blood warm. Sipping hot tea is dissipation. Drinking ice water, except in little sips, to act as a tonic, is folly. The health of many a stomach has been ruined by eating an excessive quantity of ice cream. One table spoonful should be a full allowance.

"When the body is hot and exhausted, bathe the hands and feet and face in cold water, and drink something hot. A little sweetened water, gingered, is excellent. After restoring the tone of the body to its natural condition, you may have a pleasant, healthful tonic, in a glass of ice water.

"The temptation to use stimulating drinks, is their present agreeable stimulating effect. But with every indulgence, the power to produce that sensation diminishes, until at length the stomach becomes so accustomed to their use, it would take a whole Niagara of rum to produce the sensation caused by the first glass."

"Why, Lillie," said Mrs. Savery, "are those extracts from books you have been reading?"

"Not altogether. You and father have always told me to read books to get ideas. I extract sentiments, and add reflections. What

I read, sometimes serves as a text for a sermon I preach to myself. Is there anything wrong in what I have read, or in giving the ideas of others in my own words?"

"Not exactly. I thought that expression about a Niagara of rum, sounded a little extravagant; and I understood you that you had been selecting passages from Miss Beecher's work, and I did not recollect anything like it. It sounds a good deal more like one of Henry Ward Beecher's strong similes. Read on."

"Those who use stimulating drinks, argue that the taste is a natural one, and call savages and even animals for witnesses, and therefore claim that it is right to indulge the taste; else, they say, why did God implant it in our nature. The murderer might just as well argue that to kill was no sin, because he has a natural propensity for blood.

"Stimulants were created for medicine, to cure diseases, not create them. There is not a doubt that coffee, and in some measure tea, taken in extravagant quantities as they are in this country, cause much of the nervous diseases that affect females, and all persons of natural delicate constitutions.

"Water is the only safe drink. Sugar and juice of fruits, slightly acid, may be safely added. We all drink too much. It is only a habit; it is not necessary. Children in school should not be allowed the idle habit of continually running out for a drink. If they are dry, they should be told the cause of it, and a slight punishment of thirst for eating salt to excess, will not hurt them. It may teach them to eat less. Some persons are constantly eating cloves, cinnamon, mace, orange peel, or some other spicy thing, which only serves to create thirst. No condiment with food can possibly do any good. If it stimulates the appetite to eat more, that is not beneficial. A person will soon get so he cannot eat without some stimulant.

"In this country the bulk of our food is of a stimulating nature. We consume a vast amount of meat. It is neither economical or healthy. Dyspepsia prevails here to a greater extent than in any other civilized country. Savages, owing to their nature and modes of life, and exposure of the whole body to the atmosphere, can eat meat, even whale blubber, with impunity. We must mix crude vegetables with our meat and fine flour. Of the latter we eat too much. If two-thirds of our wheat was eaten unbolted, we should enjoy better health. At one time the army bread of England was all made of unbolted wheat, and the soldiers never were so robust and healthy before or since. Those who use wheat grits, that is cracked wheat, are never constipated in the bowels. Oat meal is equally beneficial. It makes very pleasant, healthy bread. It is mostly eaten in gruel, or oat meal porridge.

"There is a great lack of economy in most families in clothing; and it is not at all uncommon that health and life are sacrificed to Moloch by fond mothers, through the folly of pride to follow the fashion of dress.

"The rule should be to cover the body, particularly of

children, so as to keep it just warm without inducing perspiration. Children often throw off their night covering, because too warm, and then suffer from exposure. This may be guarded against by using night gowns, and never covering them too warm at first.

"One person requires more clothes than another, yet all dress nearly alike. Women need thicker clothing than men, as a general thing, yet they almost always dress much thinner. Unless they wear rubbers over their shoes, their feet are as unprotected from damp or cold, as though entirely bare. They go out bare-footed, bare-headed, bare-necked, bare-armed, carrying a dragging weight of sweat cloths suspended from the hips.

"Such is woman's winter fashion.

"Men, not only in winter, but in broiling August, encase themselves in thick, solid patent-leather boots, impervious to air more than water, and black coat, vest and pantaloons, with a dozen folds of cloth around the neck, the whole topped off with a black hat, as stiff as a stove-pipe, impervious to air, and spoiled by the first dash of rain.

"Such is the economy of fashion.

"One of the most healthy practices is to wear flannel next the skin. It is a bad conductor of heat, and keeps the body warm. Black should never be worn in the sun in hot weather, because it conducts the heat to the body.

"Whatever is worn next the skin should be often changed. Cleanliness promotes health. All dresses for men, or women, or children, should be worn loose. Clothing should always be adapted to the occupation of the wearer, and colors always plain and suited to age, sex or complexion. How would the minister look with a yellow coat, or his wife with a red gown.

"One of the domestic virtues of rural life is early rising. In cities there is a certain degree of snobbishness that affects late hours at everything. These persons are late at church, late at meals, late to bed, and very late in getting out of it. It is impossible for such a late family to be healthy, and if engaged in business they are rarely prosperous. Laying in bed till the sun is two or three hours high, is very poor economy. It is poor economy to sleep by daylight and work or read by lamplight. No living thing flourishes healthily in darkness or artificial light, except sleeping.

"The fashion of dining after dark, and supping at midnight, and going to bed in the morning, is one that democratic Americans, who pretend to despise everything foreign and aristocratic, should utterly repudiate.

"Without a good reason, it should be held as a mark of a want of respectability in any woman to be out of bed at midnight.

"The unhealthiness of the night air in malarious regions, is such that it cannot be breathed with impunity in the night time. This fact is so well understood in the neighborhood of Charleston, South Carolina, that night trains upon the railroad are avoided. I have known a whole car load of passengers all sick while coming over the fifty miles of miasmatic country north of that city, in summer.

"All persons require six to eight hours sleep, and there is no better time the year through to take that, than between nine in the evening and four or five in the morning.

"All long-lived people are habitual early risers. We can, if accustomed to it, perform more labor early in the morning, than at any other period. No mother, or mistress of a family, should ask her children or hired help to get up hours before she does herself. Let her own example be a good one.

"There is no economy in late hours in bed.

"The health of many a person—women in particular—has been ruined for want of judicious exercise. Half the cases of dyspepsia, crooked spine, and nervous debility, come from want of exercise. But exercise should always have an interest for the mind. Walking merely for the exercise of walking, is fatiguing in many cases, where, if the mind was exercised also, no fatigue would be felt. Take children out in the field to hunt flowers or fruit—never to hunt bird's nests—that is all wrong—and they rarely grow tired. An invalid, who is fatigued in going up and down stairs, will climb a mountain for the view of the beautiful landscape spread out before him. All females should accustom themselves to take long walks—walks that have an object and interest for the mind. I knew one person restored to health who thought herself in a decline, just through an interest she took in a little girl, and by following her home to see her sick mother, became so interested that she walked a mile every day upon her mission of mercy and thus saved her own life.

"It was not only the exercise and fresh air, but the soothing influence of doing an angelic act to one of her own sex, who was in deep distress.

"All well trained minds feel happy when thus employed.

"The fashions of society which condemn young girls to confinement to books and a sedentary life, are destructive of beauty, grace, health and happiness.

"One of the great defects in family education is the ill-breeding of children ; that is, a want of proper training of their manners towards superiors, and touching their conduct in all the little proprieties of life.

"Be courteous, should be a daily maxim, impressed upon every child's mind. A child that is not courteous to a parent, is not one that meets with love from all. A child never should address a parent like an equal. Every one should behave at home and abroad exactly alike. If children are allowed to be rude at home, they will be so abroad. The natural disposition of children, is to assume airs of equality with those who are their seniors, and entitled to their respect and deference. If that disposition is not checked, they grow pert, overbearing, unamiable, ill-mannered. Children should be taught gratitude. 'Thank you, ma'am,' costs nothing, but it often sounds as though it was worth something.

"Never make rude remarks of another, or laugh at a defect of speech, or person, or mock an unfortunate.

"Rudeness at table is never forgiven. Nothing is more disagreeable to a well bred person. Study to imitate such persons, and you may soon be like them. Their company is always appreciated and courted, while that of a rude person is dreaded and avoided.

"A mild tempered, well bred child, no matter how homely the countenance, will always be loved and welcomed among adults or children, while one of rude manners will be excluded—perhaps hated.

"A good temper, particularly in a housekeeper, who has charge of a family, is one of the greatest blessings. It makes of itself an atmosphere of love, that glows and shines upon all the household.

"There is no purgatory more irritating to a husband than a scolding wife, or more heart-burning to a wife than a fretful husband. In such a house, how can children grow up with happy, cheerful dispositions. They feel a dread, a sort of shock, at the very step of such a parent approaching. I have seen men who never were satisfied with a meal—something was always wrong. I have seen women who apparently never spoke a good-natured word. Their words were like oil of vitriol—burning every ear they fell upon. Under their influence the husband grows discontented and unhappy, and avoids home. The children grow up ungovernable, petulant, unamiable ; a dread to others, and misery to themselves. At table, they eat more like pigs than well-behaved children, and if there are strangers in the house, the children, and the thought how they may conduct themselves, are a source of constant anxiety and dread. They are under no control, because they are the victims of a scold."

"Ah, Lillie," said Salinda, "I see you have been getting acquainted with the family of Royden's, in Father Bright Hopes. In that case both father and mother were scolds ; it is therefore no wonder the children were uncontrollable."

"And I see," said Mr. Savery, "that Lillie

has had a very good assistant in making up her composition. I am quite interested. Have you any more, my daughter?"

"Yes, sir; but I was just going to ask you if I should go on. I am afraid I shall tire you all out, with my crudities."

"I will answer for them, sister," said Frank; "when they are tired they will begin to yawn or go to sleep while you are reading.

I am thinking, father, that mother had about as much to do with this composition as sister. I wish we could have it printed; for I think it would do good to a great many other families."

"No doubt, my boy; but let us listen what more she has for us, as it is not late yet."

Lillie proceeded with cheerfulness, being thus encouraged. She even felt proud that a part of it was attributed to her mother, though she had never seen it—it was only her ideas, often instilled into a susceptible mind. She read on.

"One of the best rules of household economy is order, system, regularity. Have fixed hours for meals, and if you have servants, make them understand that every meal must be as regularly on the table, as though the starting of a railroad train depended upon it. Otherwise you will have collisions all day. Make punctuality the household law. If a child is not punctual at meal-time, fasting will soon cure the fault. Some girls in the kitchen are never punctual with meals. Don't scold. Tell them mildly what will be the consequence, at the first failure; and the second, remind them that the offence cannot be repeated with impunity; and give a prompt dismissal for the third failure.

"A gentleman who had been the torment of his first wife in never coming to his meals when ready, married a second one who was made up of clock-work. She found remonstrance was useless; but she ascertained that he was a very close calculator of dollars and cents, and she adopted this plan. She opened an account, and charged him with the time of every member of the family, every minute they were delayed by his neglect. She also charged the deterioration of dishes and loss of food by standing till they got cold and sodden; for she had everything put upon the table at the exact moment.

"At the end of a month she laid the bill upon his plate one morning. The man was astounded. His face flashed fire, but his eye rested upon a smile on the face of his wife. 'Don't you think,' said she, 'that that is a sum worth saving?' 'Wife,' said he, 'if you will allow me a credit for every day I am punctual hereafter, equal to the daily charge here, I will try to balance this account.' One month from that day she gave him a receipt in full. 'In fact,' said she, 'I think there is still a small balance in your favor. Here it is.' And she threw her arms around his neck and kissed him fondly. 'So much,' said he, 'for learning me the value of punctuality.'

"It is very bad economy to neglect the opportunity of leisure moments in every household, to cultivate the intellect. If possible, there should be an allotment of a portion of every day, where there are children, to make them know one thing more than they knew the day before.

"The father as he comes from the field may pick up three stones, by which he can teach them the names and character of three kinds of rock. Here is the hard granite, called a primitive rock ; and here is still harder quartz ; and here is the limestone that was perhaps trickling as a liquid over the others, centuries after they were formed.

"The mother as she picks the cowslip—the tender dock —the young shoots of cokeberry plant—the pig-weed or lamb's quarter—the purslain—the star plant—for greens, in the spring season, could give her children useful lessons in botany. So of every flower and fruit through summer ; teach them their formation, properties and use.

"Almost every country housekeeper knows that the bark of the common elder is medicinal; but there are two who believe it must be scraped up or down, I forget which, or it loses all its virtue, to one that knows why, or what healing power it possesses. Stew the bark in lard, no matter which way it was scraped, and it will make a healing ointment for all sores.

"Carrots prepared in the same way, make an ointment, perhaps, that excels all others for old sores. What housekeeper who thinks carrots indispensable in soup, ever thinks to inquire why they are so? Much more, if she knows, to teach her children that it is because they contain an excess over other vegetables of pectic acid, which assists to gelatinize that property of the meat in the liquid, and render the soup richer.

"How many know when they read of the okra plant, what it is, or that its pods furnish one of the richest vegetable substances that grow, for soup?

"Botany; household botany; botany of food-bearing plants, if taught children, would enable many persons to live far more comfortably and healthily than they do in their ignorance.

"A better knowledge of botany would promote the cultivation of flowers, and offer an endless source of amusement and enjoyment to children; besides promoting their health. It would be a true source of economy. It would use up little waste portions of time.

"The use and value of money should be early taught to children. One of the most effectual ways to do this is to learn them, as far as may be, to make their own purchases, and to keep an account of the cost of everything purchased for them. This should be footed up every year, and thus a young lady who never earned a dollar, might see how many she had cost. Such an account, too, would serve her as a guide to know how much many useless articles had cost, and how soon a little income could be absorbed in flimsy dresses.

"It is poor economy for a woman to spend days and weeks upon a piece of ornamental needlework, and at the same time hire her plain sewing done. It is generally poor economy to hire work done that you could just as well do yourself.

"Cheap articles are not always economical ones I knew a family who furnished a house with cheap furniture. In three years the carpets had all to be replaced. A set of parlor chairs and sofa had cost twenty-five per cent. of the original price in repairs. A cheap piano had been sent back, and a new one bought. And so on of all the articles in the house. An addition of fifty per cent. to the first cost, would have been fifty per cent. saved.

"No one, whether rich or poor, whether owner or not, has a right to destroy anything that would be useful to another.

"'I can do as I please with my own,' is false philosophy. Property is a loan of Providence that we must account for strictly. If you have an old garment that you do not want, some one else of God's creatures does; and you have no right wantonly to destroy it because you are the acknowledged owner.

"The gift of an old coat may sow the seed that will ripen you a valuable field. An old bed-quilt that you have cast aside, may save a poor woman from a fit of rheumatism; or that pair of old boots, if given to some poor boy instead of being thrown into the fire, might enable him to go to school, and afterwards perhaps to Congress, or what would be still better, become a useful mechanic.

"Economy in all expenditures is not parsimony. A man or woman may be saving, without being niggardly. A person may be generous without being lavish. Carelessness of expense is no mark of wealth or respectability. And certainly a mean disposition to cheapen, and beat down the price of goods, or hire cheap labor, is not a mark of a generous mind.

"Some persons are afraid to say, 'I cannot afford it.' They forget that is the highest recommendation of credit. It is no mark of want of money—it is an evidence of prudence in expenditures.

"Many a family have been ruined because the husband could not say to some extravagant demand of his young wife, who had never learned the value of money, or the ruin of following a foolish fashion, 'I can't afford it.'

"To a demand of some poor suffering widow, however, for a trifling assistance, a great many of those most guilty of extravagance, are ready to say, 'I can't afford it.'

"No person can afford to be sick, and therefore the art of preserving health should be constantly taught in all families and schools. It is not generally taught in churches, for of all other places they are the worst ventilated. Many of our school-rooms too, are the hot-beds where the seeds of disease are planted. Few nurseries are nurseries of health. Bed-rooms are places where the living are entombed. Neither body nor mind can enjoy health without a constant contact with pure air.

"The best advice in regard to the management of servants and children, is to avoid fault-finding. It never cures the fault. If pleasant words and good advice will not do it, you may as well give up. Don't fret whenever you find that those you have directed to do certain work, have not the judgment of yourself, or have lacked energy, or failed to execute your orders. Inexperienced minds lack forethought. They do not lack sensitiveness when chided for a fault. If the chiding is oft repeated—perhaps when least deserved—the ear grows dull and mind hardened, and instead of reform, a fixed carelessness ensues.

"There is economy as well as humanity, in the care of the sick; for with a proper care the patient may recover, instead of lingering through a long confinement. The disease of the mind is often equal to that of the body, and requires constant watchfulness and cheerfulness on the part of those in charge. It is well said that recovery depends more upon the nurse than the physician. A good nurse will always keep a room well ventilated, and in neat order. To some minds, it is a cause of deep distress when sick to see everything in confusion.

"Never ask a sick person what he or she would like to have to eat; but provide some little delicacy that is suitable, and bring it on a waiter covered with a clean napkin, and only such a minute quantity as will be sufficient, and not sicken the weak stomach at the sight of so much that cannot be eaten.

"There is nothing more valuable in a sick-room than chloride of lime. It keeps the atmosphere healthy, even in such horrid diseases as the small-pox.

"For a convenient cheap disinfector, coffee is the most readily used and quick in its action, and rarely offensive to any one. Put a few grains upon any hot iron, and roast it in the room from which you wish to remove the effluvia. In a moment you will smell nothing but the coffee. Copperas, dissolved and sprinkled about is a good disinfector. Care must be taken not to let it fall upon white cloth, as it makes a permanent stain. Acids are used for disinfectors, but the smell to some persons is disagreeable. We know one who would rather smell a skunk than vinegar fumes while heated. Burnt sugar makes an agreeable smell, and so does the smell of burning rosin; but delicate lungs may be offended with the smoke.

"I shall only mention two or three specifics, and that only because but little known.

"In small-pox, the pits can be entirely prevented, by covering the pustules as fast as they break, with a coating of collodian, a liquid cuticle, sold at all the drug shops. In malignant erysipelas, a poultice of cranberries will effect a cure when all other remedies fail.

"In all bowel complaints, the only certain remedy, that is worthy the name of specific, is a tea made of the bark of the sweet gum tree (*Liquid Amber*), that grows all over the United States, south of latitude 41°. It is an invaluable medicine for children.

"But the best medicine, and the best nurse in the world, is the one that prevents rather than cures sickness.

"Under the head of preventives, for they are promoters of health, I would rank family amusements. These, where well conducted, prepare the body and mind for the actual duties of life. Some children need amusement as much as they need food. If every father would play cards with his son, and at the same time teach him the evils of gambling, and the contempt of all respectable people for such an occupation, the gambling trade would soon cease to exist.

"But I do not by any means recommend card-playing. It is an idle game, from which nothing of practical utility is to be learned. Many other games belong to the same category. Some, however, that appear childish to a man, may be very properly indulged in by children. Rolling ten-pins; pitching quoits; skating; playing ball; are all manly exercises, but all may be indulged in by girls with advantage to the development of their physical strength, and without detriment to their morality.

"Dancing for amusement, and not for dissipation, should not be placed under the ban of the strictest moralist.

"Singing for amusement should be encouraged, and extensively practiced by all families. So should practice upon musical instruments.

"In-door amusements for children—home plays—inducements to spend the evenings at home—should be constantly studied by every parent. The most feasible, and the one which should be kept the most prominent, is family reading, and family lectures, where all are made to feel an interest in the reader, or speaker, or his subject.

"A great deal of useful labor may be done in every family, not as labor, but as a source of amusement, by which the mind is employed. Such is the cultivation of a garden. Few children, who have become accustomed to tending a garden, would be willing to dispense with it, because it is their amusement. It is their happiness to see the flowers and fruit grow ; and they show them to their companions with as much satisfaction as the builder of a ship would show his work to a company of merchants.

"In all things encourage your children to amuse themselves with something useful ; but if they strike upon a vein of mirth, or something ridiculous, do not restrain their laughter. Laugh and grow fat, is a meaning proverb. Laughter expands the lungs and promotes health. Do not tell a child that it is wicked to laugh. Learn them not to laugh at wicked stories, or stale, vulgar jokes, and never to be boisterous. Let them be merry. Let the little girl laugh with her doll, and not tell her it is 'so childish,' and that 'she ought to be ashamed of herself'—and to 'try and see if she can't be a lady.' Depend upon it, she will ape the lady soon enough without any hot-house cultivation of the faculty of imitation.

"One of the early habits that should be taught children, is to take care of their own clothes; and boy or girl, as soon as big enough, should learn to mend, and the value of that old adage, 'a stitch in time saves nine.'"

"There is another thing that children should learn," said Lillie, closing her book, and rising, "and that is the habit which I have acquired from the good example of my parents, not to continue my reading till I tire out my audience, or until it is past our usual hour of retirement. It is bed-time. You must forgive me one and all if I have trespassed upon good breeding, in my anxiety to finish in one evening, what has occupied me a month in preparing."

Mr. Savery expressed his high satisfaction at her successful production, and Salinda declared that she had learned more than she ever did before from any lecturer of the many she had listened to. Mrs. Savery, owing to the suspicion that she was partly entitled to the authorship, said nothing. Not so with Frank.

"Now, sister Lillie, that is all very good, so far as it goes; but only think how much better it would be if it was printed in a nice book, which might be read by thousands in all coming years."

That idea embodied a thought. "It is worth thinking about," said Mrs. Savery.

It is worth thinking about, whether the readers of this book are satisfied; and, if like Salinda, they think they have learned more than from the discourse of a lecturer of much higher pretensions than this school-girl, they should also think to whom they are indebted for it. Primarily, to be sure, to the writer, but certainly to Frank Savery; for it is owing to his suggestion of "how much better it would be," that it is here printed in this nice book, to be read by whole generations of such good children as Salinda, Lillie and Frank.

CHAPTER V.

Saturday—Salinda in the Kitchen—Preparation for Sunday —Visit to the Country.

SATURDAY in the Savery family, Salinda found to be what it should be in the family of all Christendom—preparation for a day set apart for cessation from labor—devotion—rest throughout all the nations that worship God through Christ.

By special invitation she spent the forenoon in the kitchen. Susan was preparing food for Sunday, so as to avoid cooking as far as possible. With that view she made a large, plain rice-pudding. It was a common-sized milk-pan full.

"I do this," said she, "because a rice-pudding is really better cold than hot, and this will serve to-morrow and Monday also; for then I shall be busy washing, and Mrs. Savery will get the dinner."

"No; that I intend to do myself, if you and she are willing."

"Certainly, with all my heart; and I can tell you everything while I am at work just as well. I always put raisins in rice-puddings, because they add a nice flavor. I generally cut them, and put them in soak over night, or a few hours before using; but you must be careful to use the water as well as fruit. I put my cinnamon in soak with the raisins, as I always use whole sticks, and if it is put in the rice dry it does not always give up all the strength. I soak my rice soft, before I mix it with the milk. It should bake slowly about two hours."

"What are you soaking this meat for?"

"That is the edge bone of the round—the most economical piece of meat in the whole beef. I shall boil that directly, till it is nice and tender, and in the liquor I shall put all that pan of roast meat bones, which I have been saving all the week, and add my vegetables, and make such a nice pot of soup—and, as you see, all for nothing. That soup is for to-morrow. You must be careful never to let soup cool in the iron pot in which it is cooked. I take it out and pour it through the cullender into the soup tureen. It sometimes, particularly if I use a good many carrots, gelatinizes so as to be like a jelly. This I heat up to-morrow in a clean tin kettle.

"The meat I shall take out, and while it is wet, I sprinkle it all over with pulverized cracker or rusk bread, with whatever seasoning is agreeable to the family. Some use garlic or onions, and various herbs. We prefer everything plain. I use a little salt, pepper, thyme, and afterwards garnish with parsley. This meat I put in a dish in a hot oven, just long enough to brown the outside. You will say to-morrow that it is very nice, and quite as good as though it was hot. This also serves for Monday, dinner and tea, and very like for breakfast Tuesday. My potatoes I prepare to-day, by boiling and mashing, and putting in this tin pan. If I have a fire in the range, I clap the pan in the oven, first glazing the top with the white of an egg. It browns and heats through directly. If I use nothing but this little charcoal furnace, I put the pan in this little bake-oven, first heating the lid, and set the whole over the coals. This and the soup is all that I have to cook. When potatoes are better fresh boiled, I can boil a mess and heat my soup with a quart of coal.

"To-morrow we shall have for dinner, cold meat and cold rice-pudding, and hot soup and potatoes, with lettuce and radishes. Perhaps Mr. Savery will bring a lobster this evening."

"And what about breakfast? Do you cook for breakfast?"

"Very little. I make a cup of tea, or cocoa. If I have cold potatoes I fry them. Then, with a little cold boiled ham, or corn beef, or tongue, or leg of mutton, with fruits in their season, we make a nice Sunday breakfast, without roasting the cook's face for it. To-morrow morning we shall have strawberries, and bread and butter, and cottage-cheese; all but the bread, fresh from Mr. Savery's mother's farm, a few miles out of town. The old lady has written that she would send them, but all hands are going out this evening for a ride, and to get these luxuries. I don't know as I ought to have mentioned it, as I believe they wanted to give you a little surprise, but I forgot that. But you see I shall have no cooking to-morrow morning, and very little all day."

"How admirably you have everything arranged so as not to interfere with the Sabbath, and yet you will have a better and far more wholesome breakfast and dinner, than many that are obtained by toil and privations of all the privileges and enjoyments of that day. But how about tea? What do you provide for that?"

"For to-morrow I shall make a nice custard, This, with the cottage-cheese—or, as some call it, smear-case—and radishes, with bread and butter, and a bit of the cold beef, if any one wants it, will make a nice hearty meal. Sometimes, in warm weather, I make the tea when I have fire, in the fore part of the day, and cork it tight in a bottle, and then I put it in the tea-pot over a spirit-lamp, and heat it in five minutes, so that I have no fire at all in the afternoon. Last summer we got in the habit of taking the tea iced, and really thought it better than when hot."

While these arrangements were going on in the kitchen, preparatory to Sunday, Frank was as busy as a bee in the garden, and Lillie, with her long coarse apron, and snug cap, was all over the house, sweeping and dusting, and "setting things to rights." Mrs. Savery was industriously engaged upon a summer coat for her husband, for it was his boast that he had never worn one made by any other hands since he was married, and that no man went neater dressed than himself.

After dinner, Mr. Savery said to his wife, "What time shall we start? I told Henry to bring the wagon round at two o'clock. Will you all be ready?"

Mrs. Savery thought he had better take the girls and Frank, and leave her, she had so much to do.

"That is the very reason why you should go. There is nothing that enables us to do so much as an occasional day of rest—a little recreation, or relaxation from labor."

Mrs. Savery said, "It would not be a day of rest to her, for she should come home much more tired than though she remained."

"Even so; and still it will be beneficial to you. No doubt you will feel fatigued, but you will sleep all the sounder, and feel refreshed in the morning, much more than though you had not taken the ride in the fresh air. Your work here will be more fatiguing than the ride."

"Suppose you let me stay, and take Susan. I am sure she needs it more than me. Poor girl, she has little chance of recreation. Her task is work, work, day after day."

"And pray, what is yours different from mine, except that you work and have the care, while I have none. I am able and willing to work, and very contented. I don't feel as though I should be willing to change places with you or any other mistress of a family. And I don't think that any sensible girl would, if every mistress would treat their servants as you do."

"Susan," said Mr. Savery, "if all girls were like you, with sense enough to know when they are well off, there would be fewer unhappy, discontented, fretful mistresses of families. Many who marry are no more fit for the station they assume, than my horse that

Henry has just driven up to the door. So now to end the difficulty as to which shall go, I will take you all. Come, hurrah, get ready."

However, Susan concluded, with her cooking on hand, that she could not leave, and would not consent that either of the others should stay in her place, though both of the girls urged her to accept their services.

It was a plain open wagon with two seats. Salinda begged the privilege of sitting with Mr. Savery on the forward one, that she might learn to drive. This he was pleased to give her an opportunity to do, because, said he, "I look upon it as a part of the education of a girl that never should be overlooked, though it generally is, that she should learn horsemanship. Every one should be taught how, so that upon emergency, if not for pleasure, she could take charge of a horse, or a pair."

"My sister Clara, then, suits your ideas exactly," said Mrs. Savery. "She can, if necessary, go to the stable and hitch up her horse —sometimes she does a pair—and take the children or a companion into the wagon, and drive off a dozen miles; and she takes pride in driving by everybody on the road. She is perfectly fearless and independent with a horse, either in a wagon or when she is on his back."

"It truly is an accomplishment," said Salinda, "that I should feel proud of; and one that I will acquire, if Charley keeps a horse. There is something excitingly pleasant, in guiding a noble animal like this along a good road. Do you think I could make myself a good driver?"

"There is not the least doubt of it. You have the very first requisite for it."

"What is that?"

"A calm temper, and freedom from that nervous impatience which runs out to the very finger ends of some people, and keeps them constantly twitching at the reins, or using the whip, or speaking sharply to urge the horse forward. Such driving will spoil any horse. The temper of the driver always seems to me to affect the horse. If one is gentle, the other is. A horse soon learns to know his driver, and frequently there is a warm affection grows up between them. Scolding and twitching a horse will spoil him as sure as the same treatment will spoil a child. This horse is gentle and playful, yet spirited. I never knew him play a trick with a woman or child. A man or boy whom he does not know had better keep his eyes open. He would soon learn to know you. He would distinguish the very touch of your hand on the rein, it is so steady and firm, without pulling. Your voice, too, is soft; a horse is as easily charmed by such a voice, as a man. There is great magnetic power in the human voice."

"What makes him prick up his ears now and start forward?"

"It is because his ear is quicker than yours or mine. There is another horse on the road, and he hears him coming round the bend, and is not disposed to be passed. Now you hear what he heard at first."

"Oh, will he want to run to keep ahead?" said Salinda, with a slight suspicion that her horsemanship might be insufficient in a race.

"Not unless you wish him. He is ready for a word of command. Speak to him as you give a gentle, though sudden, pull on the bit.

Ned, steady, sir. You see how easily he subsides. Ah, there they come; a dashing pair of pampered greys, and open barouche, with driver in livery."

"Oh, father," said Lillie, looking back, "it is the Doolittles, with their new turn-out. Mrs. D., Kitty, and Triphenia, with her bearded beau."

"Has Doolittle bought that establishment?" said Mr. Savery. "The man is crazy. I understand now how it is that Tom Whip was hawking Doolittle's notes for fifteen hundred dollars, through the streets, at twenty-five per cent. discount. A man doing a business certainly not worth over two thousand dollars a year—a mere mechanic—and a hard-working, honest mechanic, too—for that is Doolittle's character, if it is not his name—to buy a fifteen hundred dollar carriage and horses, just to gratify his weak-minded, vain wife, and badly-educated, proud daughters—the thought is sickening. Poor Doolittle! the best wish that I can give him, in all honesty of heart, for I do feel that I am an old friend, is that he may never live to see the ruin that is rapidly coming upon his family. No mortal hand can avert it. If the Maine law had been in force ten years ago, his reasoning faculties might have been saved. Without being thought a drinking man, he has taken enough to ruin his intellect, and leave him an easy prey to the folly of his gad-about, do-nothing, instead of Doolittle, wife. The man is ruined."

It is not likely that the load of jewel-bedizzened pride that swept by in their velvet-cushioned, easy carriage, as they looked out from the cloud of silks and laces, upon the occupants of that humble wagon, had an idea that the time would ever come to them again, when they would be obliged to travel in so mean a conveyance, as a plain one-horse buggy.

"Oh, Kitty! for mercy sake give me my smelling-bottle, or I shall faint;" said Triphenia, as their carriage swept by, bringing her as she sat forward, almost face to face with Salinda.

"Dear me!" said her mother and sister, "what is the matter? You look pale. We had better drive back to town at once—the country air never agreed with Triphenia—she is *so* delicate."

She was eighteen, and weighed a hundred and thirty-five, and if she looked pale, it was the pale of fuller's earth or pearl white. She was too much affected to answer her mother's anxious inquiries after her health, and so Mr. George Alexander Waltringham, the "gentleman from the South," ventured to suggest that "those vulgar people in that wagon—that one-horse wagon—had pretended to try to recognize her as an acquaintance, which had shocked her very susceptible nervous system. There was a very bold, forward, pert young miss, some country gawky, I suppose, sitting on the forward seat with a common-looking sort of man, driving the horse, while he took it easy. We never see such things in Georgia. I think it was the vulgar look of the thing that made her feel faint."

"Yes, mother; and I think you would have fainted too, if you had seen what I did. That girl that George Alexander describes so correctly, was Salinda Lovewell, driving that old lumber wagon of the Saverys, with the whole family packed up together. Don't you think the merchant's daughter is coming down in the world? I hope you don't blame us now for cutting her acquaintance. I really don't know what the world is coming to. I could not have believed it if I had not seen it with my own eyes. It is enough to make any one feel faint, who knows what good society is."

Good society!! Heaven bless us! Five years ago, the Doolittle family would have been very glad to ride in as good a wagon with a borrowed horse. Now they rolled away in a very atmosphere of their own, that shut out all reminiscences of scenes of early life and old acquaintances.

Doolittle himself was an honest, hard-working mechanic, but lacking that stability of mind which would have enabled him to resist the outside pressure of a weak-minded, proud woman, who was bringing up her children in idleness and frivolity, he had been forced to abandon a comfortable country home, for a fashionable city residence and an expensive mode of living, that, notwithstanding his large increase of business would lead him to one inevitable result—one that sooner or later overtakes every one who lives beyond his income.

For a man, situated as Doolittle was, to buy a pair of horses and carriage, Savery looked upon as only one remove from insanity.

"I do not envy them," said Salinda, as they sailed away past the humble, yet very comfortable wagon in which she was riding.

"You need not," replied Mr. Savery, "but they will you, if all of you live five years. Have you ever visited the family?"

"I have not, though frequently urged to do so by Mrs. Doolittle and the girls, who often call upon my mother. I don't know that I should be welcome now, as I was told they intended to cut my acquaintance, after, as they said, I had turned kitchen girl"—

"For the Saverys. Put it all in; we heard of it, but did not feel offended," added Mrs. Savery. "Depend upon it, if we should call there, we should be in danger of being eaten up if we were sugar, they would be so sweet upon us."

"I wish, wife, that you would try it; as

everything is judged by contrast, it would be well for Salinda to learn how others live, as well as those she is associated with."

"Oh, there is grandmother," exclaimed Frank, a good deal more interested in looking ahead for the first sight of that much honored old lady, than anything his father and mother were saying about the Doolittles, or anybody else.

Mrs. Whitlock was a lady in the true meaning of that term. She was of the old Puritan stock. For a dozen years she had been a widow, but in all that appertained to the management of the farm, a scrutinizing neighbor said he could see no change since her husband's death.

Mr. Whitlock was a man of rare good sense. Years before his death, he made his will. It was short and pertinent. "My wife," he said, "has been thirty years my partner in business, and in company we have accumulated some property. If she dies first, the law gives me the entire management, without noticing her death any more than it would the death of my horse. If I die first, she is accounted by law as nobody, and barely permitted to have a little portion of what I leave. All the property must be sold, whether anybody wishes it or not. The sanctuary of the house is invaded by strangers, to make an inventory of all I may leave behind. The law does not permit my old partner to carry on my old business, for the benefit of our children, or creditors. The concern must be broken up. Such is the law. Therefore, I make a will. This the law must execute. I constitute my aforesaid partner, my sole heir, executor, and guardian of my children and property. I trust she will continue the partnership business, if she deems it advisable, just so long as she considers it profitable, and that she will pay all my debts, and dispose of my property, which will then be solely hers, in just such a manner as she sees proper."

Every man that has such a wife, should make such a will.

Mrs. Whitlock was in the front porch when the wagon drove up. It was such an unusual thing for her to come out to see a carriage pass, that she felt as though she must apologize for such an idle curiosity.

The children could hardly wait for the wagon to stop, before they were out, and through the gate, and up the steps, to give grandmother the first kiss. Mr. and Mrs. Savery both greeted the old lady in the same way. The children came naturally by their affectionate dispositions.

"And this," said the old lady, "is Nat Lovewell's daughter. I knew her mother before she was her age. I am really happy on her account, to welcome you to my house. Come in. I need not ask if you are all well —your countenances tell that."

"Oh, grandma, were you out looking for us?"

"No indeed, for I did not know you were coming. I was going to send the things down by Sam this evening. But I am very glad you have come, for now you can pick the berries yourselves; I know you will like that.

"I was out looking at that splendid carriage —no, not at the carriage, either, exactly; but Sam had been telling me about it, and just then Debby saw it coming, and insisted that I should come out and look; at the same time quoting the old proverb repeated by Sam, of 'put a beggar on horseback and he will ride to the devil.' You know Sam feels a little bitter towards the Doolittles since Triphenia jilted him for her 'Southern planter,' as she calls him, though Sam insists upon it that he is nothing but a blackleg, horse-racer, and I don't know what all. Well, well, never mind the Doolittles—I am heartily glad that my son is clear of his engagement to marry one of them, for I think they will all go to ruin.

"Now, children, you go and pick the berries, and I will get the smear-case ready, and your mother, and—what is your name? for I never can call you Miss Lovewell—may take a walk round, or sit here until I get through my work. I want you—Salinda, is it?—to feel at home, and never mind me. You are just as welcome as though I made a fuss about it."

"Can't we help you, mother, about your work?"

"Oh, la! no. I don't want any help. Debby will get the butter ready. She is working it over now. I can hear her patting with the butter ladle."

"Can't we," said Salinda, "go out among the chickens, and in the orchard, and look through the garden?"

"Oh, yes, do. You will find the calves in that lot. I do think our old yellow cow's calf this year, excels any former one. The butcher offered me twelve dollars, a week ago, but I told him that I should make it better worth fifteen. He laughed, and said he didn't doubt it. Then we have such a lot of pigs—real butter-milk pigs. Sam says they will sell in a month from now at a better profit than after they have eaten ten bushels of corn apiece. I reckon there is something in it. The true economy of farming is to sell things when they bring the most profit, not when they bring the most money. Oh, do go and look at my lambs, Jotham, you used to be so fond of lambs when you lived at home."

Finally, all the others concluded that they wanted to see the lambs and calves, and pigs, and chickens, and so they would all go together; but Mrs. Whitlock said, "You forget, children, one of my precepts. Always do your work first and play afterwards. You have your berries to pick, and you are to have just as many as you choose to gather. Better do that first."

"So we had, mother," said Mrs. Savery, "and therefore we will all go and do that, and then do our running about."

"That is very well. Many hands make light work, is another of my maxims. You know where to find the baskets, and while you are about it, you may pick enough for our tea."

She said truly, that they knew where to find the baskets. Everybody that ever knew once might know in all future time ; for everything had a place, and everything when used must be returned to its place. It was no wonder that order was the law of Mrs. Savery's house. She inherited it from her mother.

Every tree, shrub, vine, plant; all partook of the same appearance of order, neat arrangement, taste, and adaptation to their several situations.

The house was one of those old-fashioned ones, still common in New England, which, for a farm-house it is difficult to improve. The objection to them now is that since wood has grown scarce, it costs too much to keep up the fire in the great chimney in the centre of the house; upon each side of which in front, there is a "square room," one of which is the "spare room," and the other the "common room." Behind the chimney is a great kitchen, with its enormous fire-place and oven. At one end of the kitchen is the stairway, and passage to the "end door," and a buttery; and at the other end is a bed-room. There is a "settle" on one side of the fire-place, and a blue dye-tub in one corner. A long, heavy oak table stands by the windows, with a back seat, a bench fixed to the wall. There is a "lean to" behind for a milk-room and sink room, just outside of which is the great stone-walled well, where

"The old oaken bucket, the iron-bound bucket,"

dangles from the long pole and great crotch and sweep. Then comes the "clothes-yard," a broad piece of turf, as smooth as a carpet. Even here, order and economy are exhibited in saving the clothes line from the weather, or necessity of taking it down by hand and carrying it into the house. Upon the post near the well there is a little box, enclosing a wheel with a crank, with which the hundred feet of line can be wound in one minute. When it is wanted it is run out in as little time over the forks in the top of the posts, and a loop hitched over a pin at the farther end. Then a turn of the wheel and a catch tightens and holds it so.

Beyond the clothes yard and on a lower level lies the garden. A drain from the house carries all the waste water to a tank in the garden, and every rain that falls washes any little fertilizing matter on or about the house, down to the garden, where it will do good.

The house, as all country houses should do, when it is feasible, fronts the north. This gives the genial sun to the kitchen side, where it is most needed to evaporate moisture, and look into the broad kitchen windows on mid-winter day.

To the west of the garden was "the little orchard," and across the road north of the house, spread out the big orchard. In front of the house, and along both sides of the road the full length of the farm, there were two rows of trees, alternating with elms, maples, mulberry, butternut, black-walnut, and several great cherry-trees, and one very large pear-tree, and three excellent autumn apples. These were all planted by Mr. Whitlock, as he said, for the public. His children, or grand-children would see the benefit of them, and how much they would be valued. Not only his children, but himself lived to see many a panting horse reined up in the pleasant shade of some of those trees, to recuperate strength for a drive over a long sunny road.

Many a tired traveller, no doubt, sent up his thank-offering for the refreshing luxury of that way-side fruit.

Planting shade-trees and fruit-trees by the wayside, ought to be inculcated as a Christian duty.

On the east side of the house commenced the farm buildings. The first was a neat wagon-house next the road, two-stories high, the upper loft a seed-room, and place to store wool and various other things. From the wagon-house extended a long shed, where dry wood was always stored. In one end was a room called the shop, containing a carpenter's bench and tools, a portable forge, and a set of tools for mending harness, or saving a shilling by a stitch in time in a pair of shoes. At the other end was a room with a kettle set in an arch, which was used for making soap, trying out fat, and cooking food for the pigs, which occupied a pen on the other side of the building, communicating with the barn-yard beyond, or with the little orchard, where they were allowed to run, except when the fruit was ripe and falling from the trees. Connected with the pig-pen was the hen-house, and beyond that a large yard in which they could be shut whenever it was desirable to keep them out of the garden. One side of the poultry-yard was formed by the corn-crib, with an opening for them under the building, so that every grain that fell was not wasted, but was picked up by some sharp-eyed biddy, always watching for a chance grain.

"If you keep hens," said Mr. Whitlock, "under the crib, you will not keep rats or mice. It is only a question of which is most profitable."

The barn was a pattern of convenience. The milking-yard was between the wood-shed and barn. The stable-yard on the south side, the stables occupying a basement. A rise of ground on the north side, gave a roadway, by a slight inclined plane, to the second story of the barn. When a load of hay was driven in, the driver without any assistance, could hitch a tackle-block to the wagon-bed, and detach his team and hitch them to the fall, and start them forward, lifting the whole load, which then swung round by a crane over the great bay, when by a simple contrivance the ropes on one side unhooked, and down dropped the whole load. In this way, in fifteen minutes, he could unload and start out for another. Thus a hundred tons could be put under shelter without any of the hard work and heavy expense of pitching and stowing away.

One of the things that most grieved Mr. Whitlock about his barn and stable arrangements was that he had no hill-side spring that he could lead through pipes to every animal as it stood in the stall. If he had had a spring a hundred feet lower down than his stable, he could have still got a supply by means of that curious and very valuable little hydraulic machine, the "Water-ram." But his situation afforded neither one nor the other; but he did the next best thing that he could do; he made extensive cisterns near the barn, but the water had to be pumped up by hand. His spirit perhaps now looks down to see how Sam and his mother, by the aid of scientific discoveries, have obviated this difficulty. On the top of the barn is one of "Halliday's Wind Engines," a newly invented windmill, that regulates its own sails to any wind, high or low, and pumps a constant stream of water up to a reservoir in the barn, so situated that it is covered with hay in winter and never freezes, and from which water can be drawn to every stall, pig-pen, poultry-yard, and for the cows in the milking lot. It is a cheap, valuable, labor-saving machine. Its use is true economy.

"Mother," said Mrs. Savery, as they came in with their baskets full of the ripe fruit. "I have never known your strawberries so plenty and fine-flavored as this year; how do you account for it?"

"We read in the newspaper, that the strawberry bed should never be manured in any way except with decayed wood or leaves, and that spent bark from the tanner's yard was first-rate. This is the second year that we have tried it, and in addition to that, this summer, Samuel waters them with a decoction of fresh oak bark, because he read that tannic acid was necessary to give strawberries that rich flavor. The experiment has cost nothing, and the profit is incalculable. It, with the frequent waterings he gives them, will more than double the yield of the bed. By the by, that last improvement was your suggestion, Jotham; so that we can well afford to give you all that you want. Now remember, if your little bed does not give you all that you can eat, you must send out here and get a supply. It is a great deal more pleasure to me to give them to you than to sell them. Why what started Frank and Lillie off on the run? Oh, I see now, they got a glimpse of their uncle Samuel, coming through the orchard. There he is like a playful boy, down on the grass, with both of them on his lap. He will dirty Lillie's frock, I'll warrant, or some mischief. I do wish Sam was married, and had some children of his own, if he would love them as well as he does your's, Mary."

"If it warn't for one thing, mother, I could find a match that would please you."

"Oh yes, I understand, but Charley Goodman is just as good a man as Sam Whitlock, and ——— here Salinda began to get uneasy. Oh you need not blush to own such a young man as your lover. I do wish it was the fashion, as soon as a couple are betrothed, to own it to their friends, and treat each other, and be treated accordingly. It would be a very happy pleasant state of society, and often lead to better results than the present fashion. Besides it would avoid lying."

Samuel now came in, as his mother said, as rough as a bear, with his long beard, and dirty as a pig from a week's toil on the farm, yet when introduced to Salinda, in her eyes, he dropped all the roughness of the farm, for she only saw and heard, a most polite well-bred gentleman, well read, and full of intelligence upon every subject.

"Is it possible," she thought, "that this is the man that I have heard so ridiculed by the Doolittles, as Triphenia's country beau. Why he is as much superior to that fop of her's, as man is superior to a monkey."

It is well, Charley Goodman, that you are firmly seated in her heart, for there is one beneath that rough exterior that beats in unison with hers. If it was free, it might be won, for she likes the man, and is fairly in love with his country home.

What a table they sat down to about six o'clock. Strawberries and sugar, strawberries and cream, strawberries and such nice cool milk, for I forgot to mention the ice-house, one of the luxuries and economies of every farm.

Then such sweet butter and fresh-baked rye and Indian bread, and old style light biscuit.

When the butter was commended, the old lady told how she made it.

"I have tried churning sweet milk, and I have churned my cream sweet, and I have kept it till it soured. I have washed my butter, and I have made it without washing, and after all I could not lay down any fixed rule for everybody to follow. If I get every drop of buttermilk out, either by washing and working, or working alone, my butter will keep sweet a year. This was made of sweet cream, and worked once with a paddle, and salted with an ounce of fine rock salt to a pound, and a spoonful of fine white sugar,—that is Debby's notion—I don't think it hurts it any."

"And this, that you call smear case, how is it made?"

"You saw Debby, when you were in the milk-room, emptying the bonny-klauber in the brass kettle. That is brought to a scald, and the curd settles down and the whey rises. We pour off all we can, and then turn the whole out in a strainer over the whey-tub and let it drain an hour or two."

"Is that all, grandma?"

"Oh no; it is then tied up and hung away to drain all night. It is then in quite a hard cake. This we crumble up by hand, and add about a gill of cream to a quart, with a little salt, and that is smear case; it is the Dutch of soft cheese. If we want to send it to market, we make it up in little round balls and lay them between two clothes, and put a board and weight on top to press them down into little cakes, like small biscuit, and these are called cottage cheese, or Dutch cheese. Sometimes the cream is entirely omitted. It is a good wholesome food for those that like it."

"Of which I am one, said Salinda; though I never tasted any so good as this before."

"The enjoyment of eating is greatly owing to surrounding circumstances; I don't think I could relish my food as well, where I knew that neatness never had an abiding-place. This is economical food, for we only value milk after we have got the cream, for pig feed. Do you prefer that brown bread to the biscuit? That is what I call my half and half—equal parts of corn meal and rye, the bran of each only sifted out. Scald the meal and mix it thoroughly into a mush, and then add the rye, and knead it well. You can't make bread without hard work. I used to do that, but I am not strong enough now, but Debby is. She is a right good girl for strong work."

"I guess, mother, we must be going, to get home before dark."

"Well, I'spose you must. I am really 'bliged to you for this visit. I shall not urge you to stay longer, because I know its time you were going."

"Indeed Mrs. Whitlock, I think the obligation is all on our side."

"Oh no, Salinda, remember it is more blessed to give than receive. And besides, you don't know how much it does an old woman's heart good, to have her children come back to the old homestead, and sit around the same table once more. And as for you, I really wish you would come every week, or for the matter of that, every day. You have done a sight of good."

"Why how? I don't understand a word."

"I will leave it for Lillie, the young rogue, to tell you. She says: grandma, do see how uncle Sam is fixed up, all out of compliment to Salinda."

It was not that altogether, it was the natural homage and respect of a noble heart to beauty, intelligence and worth. It was the evidence of good breeding, often found under the roughest exteriors upon American farms. Sam Whitlock the farmer, would be, always will be, Samuel Whitlock the gentleman born, gentleman bred, gentleman in all that makes the character. He had in his young days fixed his heart upon a girl who as she grew up, could not understand that character, and luckily for him, concluded to break her troth, since which he had fallen into habits of indolence, as regards the exterior appearance of a gentleman. Salinda had unconsciously awakened that feeling which prompts a man to look to personal appearance, and the quick eye of his mother, as well as Lillie, saw it, and felt grateful to the object. She thought and said, "You have done a sight of good."

Just as they were going out to the wagon, the Doolittle carriage was coming down the road. Sam fairly outdid his nature, in the little courtesies of the occasion. Was there a little natural feeling, to let Miss Triphenia see that he was not utterly disconsolate? Was there on the part of Salinda, a little desire to assist him, even at the risk of being called, as she was called, "the shameless flirt." The girls would have preferred to dash by with a simple nod of recognition, but their mother either felt guilty of such rudeness, and ordered the driver to rein up, or else she saw the baskets of tempting strawberries, and was prompted to the act by a spirit of greediness. Let us hope it was not the latter. A stranger might have thought the new-comers were the warmest friends of the family, so enthusiastic was their greeting. They were so delighted to have the opportunity of meeting their old friends and neighbors all together. The girls complimented Salinda upon her skill in driving, it was "such an accomplishment."

"If we had such a lovely little snug carry-all, and only one horse—but pa would have two—we should certainly learn to drive."

How quick the wicked remarks made as they drove past, had passed into the ocean of forgetfulness.

Those remarks were to the backs, and these to the faces of those they talked about. What a happy thing our thoughts are hidden, and half our words unheard.

Samuel, as the old lady remarked, was all himself again. He was full of life, and "just as polite as ever." He was sending a pang to every heart in the Doolittle carriage. George Alexander Waltingham in his heart felt that Triphenia was a fool to throw away such a man, and such a prospect of being the mistress of a house and farm like this for a —— gambler. He almost spoke the word, so strongly he thought of it. But he covered up his thoughts with his supercilious actions, which he thought would pass well in the present company, as evidence of high breeding. Except with a fraction of the company, he was very much mistaken. The others thought him just what he was—an adventurer, a fop, a libertine. He was one of a numerous class, that pluck flowers only for their fragrance, while fresh with morning dew, and then cast them away as worthless trash.

Mrs. Whitlock and her son, both insisted upon the Doolittles stopping for some strawberries. She had already spoken a word to

Debby, and she had already reset the table, while they were making excuses for doing just what they were most anxious to do, so that by the the time they got in the house, every thing was ready for them to sit right down to such a repast as they most ardently desired, notwithstanding the repeated protestations that they "had not the least occasion in the world." And notwithstanding the girls had "cut the acquaintance" of Salinda, she was most pressingly urged to call upon them, "before they left town on their summer tour." Of course Mrs. Savery and Lillie were included in the invitation, though Kitty said she hoped "that stuck-up school-girl would have sense enough not to come." The truth was, that she felt herself the foil that added lustre to Lillie's diamonds of a cultivated mind, whenever they were brought into contrast.

"Speaking of contrast," said Mr. Savery, "I am going to show you the contrast of Mother's farm."

The man was thinking. Nobody said a word about contrast; they all thought of it though.

"It is Doolittle's father's—old Captain

Doolittle—it is only half a mile out of the way, and except the half mile, the best road, and then you will see a greater diversity of scenery too, and have more food for thought. This way. Ned knows the road."

"Do you think that Mrs. Doolittle will come this way, father," said Lillie.

"Not a bit more than she would drive through fire. I doubt whether that Mr. What-do-you-call him, will ever hear that the family ever had any American ancestors. You know they have a coat of arms, and trace back on his side to some remote baronetcy. There is not an old castle in Sir Walter Scott's novels, that some of the Doolittle family were not connected with in their opinion. But here is the last baronial hall of the family."

The house stood "back side to the road," and a very unsightly show its old wood-colored walls, and mossy roof, and broken windows made. The well was in line with the road-fence, with a horse-trough outside, and a hog-wallow beyond, that looked like the slough of despond, to any one that would approach the well from that side. This puddle extended beyond the gate, and had to be crossed on rails thrown in the mud. The gate had to be lifted around upon one hinge. It was always fastened with a pin, provided the pin was not lost, or the gate had not been rooted open by the hogs; to prevent which, three dogs stood, or rather slept guard on the portico, which contained a great assortment of old saddles, harness, hoes, rakes, wheels, loom, old coats, hats and boots, in a sort of public free exhibition.

Beyond the well, on one side, was the hog-pen, with an opening to the road; for the owner believed in the largest liberty for his stock. On the other side was an open wagon-shed, where the hens roosted, and did the ornamental work of the go-to-meeting carriage. Right in front of the gate was the wood-pile, frequently furnished with whole trees, snaked up, because the cart was broken, or the wagon had gone to mill.

The barn was right opposite the house, and the cow-yard in the road between, which, in addition to the wood-pile, was encumbered with all the broken down carts, wagons, sleds, harrows, plows, hay-racks, fence-posts, and sticks of timber, that had been or might be in use during the century. In the summer, a good part of this chevaux-de-frise was hidden from view by a rank growth of stramonium.

From the house and barn, boards had fallen, or were dangling by one nail; and the orchard looked as though nothing but the scythe of Time had ever been there as a pruning-hook.

The garden palings had been broken, and the holes stopped with brush from the snaked up trees at the wood-pile. A hole in the orchard wall was patched with an old cart-bed. One of the big doors of the barn, which Mr. Savery said had hung for a year by one hinge, had gone down at last, and was propped up sideways with a rail. An old harrow stood guard in place of a stable door, and some scraggy poles at the barn-yard did service where bars and bar-posts were both gone. A swarm of bees were at work in the old chaise-box, not having been able to get any other hive. That had deprived the old lady of the privilege of going to meeting for the balance of the summer. The garden had been made, and unmade by the hens, three times, and then given up, because "they couldn't afford to be always making garden."

It was a contrast—it was food for thought. Salinda went home a wiser as well as happier girl than she went forth. She had seen much and learned much—much that is never learned in schools. Schools that turn out mindless machines—expensive experiments to cramp reason out of its natural purpose. Schools that teach music that gives just as much accomplishment as the hand-organ possesses. Schools of design, that teach children to badly copy a bad picture. History and geography is taught just as much as the parrot is taught sense by repeating words. Schools of industry, that teach needle-work that is utterly impracticable and useless all through life. Such is fashionable education.

They found company waiting for them when they got home. Mr. and Mrs. Lovewell, and Charley Goodman, were there. The meeting was as joyful as though they had been separated for a year. Salinda's mother met her with a warm embrace. Her father with a dignified smile and formal shake of the hand. How she did wish he would press her to his breast as Mr. Savery did. She would have put her arms around Charley's neck and given him a kiss—a warm token of love—fear of being called forward held her back, and made her restrain nature. But she looked what she felt, as they shook hands. Lillie felt no such restraint, and she ran up to him and put her arms fondly around his neck, and gave him such a kiss; laughing heartily as she said to Salinda, "that is the way to do it, isn't it, Charley.";

Charley expressed his very high satisfaction at that mode of salutation, and returned it with a hearty, "God bless you, Lillie, my dear good girl. You are as fragrant as a bed of strawberries."

"No wonder, and that reminds me." She cast a look at her mother, as much as to say, Shall I? Her mother looked, Yes, and away she bounded, returning in a few minutes with a fine dish of sugared strawberries, followed by Susan with plates and spoons. It was a very grateful treat: the berries and cream both so fresh and sweet. Salinda said, "I think, father, that I can give you something that you will like, if possible, better than the strawberries."

"Oh, I know what 'tis," said Lillie, and away she ran for the smearcase. Instead of one, she brought three dishes. Mrs. Lovewell declined, but Mr. Lovewell said it was delicious. Of course, Susan had added bread and butter. Charley told Lillie that he had not tasted but one thing better since he came in the house, and that preceded the strawberries.

"You shall taste something better still before you leave. Wait and watch."

He had not to wait long. Lillie proposed that he should go and see how neat Salinda had got everything arranged up stairs. "Oh, she is getting to be a famous housekeeper. Susan and her are on great terms in the kitchen."

He did admire the neat arrangement. His heart was full. Salinda stood before him, more lovely than ever. It was an impulse of the moment that led him to do what he had so often ardently desired to do, yet dared not venture. He took her in his arms, pressed her fondly to his heart, and kissed her passionately. It was the happiest moment of her life. It was the first, as she fondly hoped, of a long series.

"My dear, dear little wife. How you do win upon my heart every day. How much I should love you."

Her head sunk upon his breast. She was in an ecstasy of delight. Tears of joy streamed down the good Lillie's cheeks, and the affection of her heart gushed out. She too felt the impulse, and she threw her arms around both, and as she kissed Salinda, said:

"Let me too be happy."

The tears of the trio mingled. There were other moist eyes, looking at this scene. Mrs. Savery and Mrs. Lovewell, had followed them up stairs, and had, unnoticed, witnessed the whole of this outgushing of nature. What mother could refrain from sympathizing with such children. Mrs. Lovewell did not chide, she only cautioned prudence. "She had no objection to this show of what their hearts felt, if only indulged in presence of some one who would be a little restraint, so that they would not act foolishly, as lovers are sometimes inclined to do. Even in affection, there should be a degree of dignity and respect. There is some truth in the old adage, that 'familiarity breeds contempt.' It is not safe for human nature to trust to good resolutions. I do not counsel coldness and reserve between an affianced couple, but such reserve as produces respect."

Mrs. Lovewell expressed a high degree of satisfaction at all of Salinda's arrangements, and what she heard of her disposition and progress in the study of the art of housekeeping: and Charley felt that she had never appeared so lovely before. He knew very well what a good teacher she had, and that she was acquiring accomplishments of the highest order for an American woman, such as no public seminary ever gives.

Of all the members of that little party that night at Mr. Savery's, it would be difficult to tell which went to bed most happy. Even Mr. Lovewell, with all his apparent coldness, had a warm heart, and was most proud of his daughter, and happy to see her happy.

CHAPTER VI.

The Visit to the Doolittles.

NOT long after the above events, Mrs. Lavery, Salinda, and Lillie, went to make their visit to the Doolittles. Of course they were received with demonstrations of great delight. The door was opened by the coachman, gardener, man of all work, and good at none—a useless appendage and foolish expense to such a family. He was attending to this duty, as Mrs. Doolittle apologized, because both of their chamber girls had suddenly left.

"They were very impertinent, asking me for their wages, time after time, instead of waiting for me to give it them when it was convenient; and, finally, this morning they told Doolittle about it, and he, the fool, gave them the money, and no quicker than they got it, they both packed up and cleared out. I do wish men would attend to their own business, and not undertake to manage our household affairs. However, I am glad they are gone, for they had got to be quite worthless. You can see that by the looks of the house."

Indeed it was easy to see that somebody was quite worthless about the house. The parlors were elegantly furnished, so far as costly frail furniture could make elegance, and that was all. There was scarcely a chair or sofa that was not broken or scratched, or torn, and every crevice showed the worthlessness of those whose business it had been to keep the furniture free of dust. Salinda counted five holes in the lace curtains, punched by dirty fingers. Perhaps they had been made by marble fingers, for several had been broken from the statuettes which ornamented the mantels. There were several grease spots upon the carpet, one of which bore unmistakable evidence of a recent fall of bread and butter. The piano was out of tune, because the "children will keep thumping at it." In short, the whole house was out of tune. About an hour after the arrival of their guests, "the young ladies" sailed down stairs, with a profusion of fancy gauze, silk, lace, ribbons, and jewelry, and their hair in such a friz as might astonish, if not frighten, one of the aborigines of the American forest. There was no need of half the lying excuses for their late appearance ; such as having so much work to do, in consequence of the departure of those ungrateful girls, and quite forgetting how late it was, and how punctual Mrs. Savery always is, and how they had to dress each other's hair. Salinda might have believed the latter, as it was impossible for either to make such a fright of herself alone, if she had not caught a glimpse of a well-known French hair-dresser, as he went down stairs.

Of course the girls could not show their proficiency in music, because the piano was out of tune. Lillie said slyly, that she never knew it otherwise. It was a standing excuse. If it ever happened to be in order, the girls always had "horrid colds."

Salinda proposed to look at the garden. They could not refuse, though it was in a "shocking condition." In that they spoke the truth. But the most shocking part of it was, that it was filled with expensive shrubs and flowers, to such a degree that there was no room for fruit, or anything beyond a few roses, of any practical use.

Tender plants were choked with grass and weeds, or trampled on by careless feet, and those of larger growth bore marks of having officiated in place of a clothes-line, and the paths were whitened with dried soap-suds. Grease, dirt, old rags, broken crockery, scraps of meat, and cooking utensils made up a slut's museum around the back basement door and windows. The full view was hidden from the garden by an untrimmed, and of course unproductive, grape-vine, that shut out the sun from the very place where it was most needed to dry up the moisture and prevent miasma.

Just as the party returned to the house, there was a tearing ring at the door-bell, and a thundering knock at the basement door at the same time. As it was doubtful which to go to first, the man took a middle course and went to neither. Directly those outside grew impatient, and began kicking the doors as though they would knock them down or force them open.

"Why don't that lazy fellow go to the door?" said one of the girls, "It is really provoking."

Why did she not herself open it when she was within three steps when the bell rang. It would have compromised her dignity. At length the lower door was opened, and by the noise, a mad bull came in, stamping with fury.

"I'll tear your eyes out, you old black nigger, if you don't open the door next time when I am starved. Where is Ned? If he's got in first, I'll lick him."

Up stairs he went to ascertain that fact. No one else being likely to let in master Neddy, Mrs. Doolittle suggested to Kitty that she might attend to it, just this once. She went off muttering about having to do servant's work. Master Ned came in uproarious, but better-natured than his fighting brother Welt—the short name of Wellington. Perhaps his fighting character was partly owing to his name. Character is often influenced by a slighter circumstance.

"Oh, you're so dressed up you couldn't come to the door, eh? I'll pay you for it some time, Miss Kitty. I won't open the door, nor let any of the rest of 'em, for your beau, and mother won't be here to make me, for you always have him come when mother is out. See if I don't."

"Do hush, Ned, you don't know who is in the parlor."

"I don't want to know. Old Whiskerandos, I s'pose; he's here all the time. I wish Phene would have him and done with it."

Mrs. Doolittle closed her ears to this interesting conversation, under the impression probably that by so doing she would close those of her visitors.

Either of his sisters could have wrung Ned's neck, without any compunctions of conscience. Now another actor, in the person of the mad bull, came tearing up the basement stairs, and "pitched in" to give Ned a licking because he got in first, and to serve Kitty in the same way for letting him in.

"He bet me his cap that he would get home first, and get in and up to the parlor door; and he cheated; he had no business to come in this way when I thought he was going to t'other door, and then we could have a fair race up stairs. But I'll have the cap anyhow."

At that he went at him to get the cap, and down they both went in the hall in a regular bull-dog, rough-and-tumble fight. Mrs. Doolittle still oblivious. Kitty had returned with a face that needed no rose pink. It was burning red, and she bit her lip to keep in the angry words that would have poured out if they had not been restrained by the company of strangers.

"Oh dear, what is that?" exclaimed Mrs. Doolittle, as a crash that jarred the house, came from the field of combat in the hall.

Instinctively all rushed out to see. A niche had been constructed in the wall at the foot of the stairs for a piece of statuary. Unfortunately it was too shallow to hold a plaster cast of some mythological goddess that the young ladies had purchased, because "the place looked so naked without something."

Somehow in the scuffle, this had been jarred so that it toppled over, and down it came upon a table, made more for ornament than use, upon which stood a Chinese vase of flowers. The whole was a wreck together. At least fifty dollars had gone into the maelstrom that was swallowing up poor Doolittle's property. The boys perfectly understood that "discretion was the better part of valor," and made a hasty retreat. The girls raged—they lost their discretion. Their mother was angry enough to have torn the boys like a tiger, but finally consoled herself for all the loss, with the thought that that nude figure had been got rid of, because "she never thought it looked decent." Mrs. Doolittle was one of those admirers of statuary, who think it should be dressed in calico frocks, or at least wear aprons. In the midst of the confusion, and just as Triphenia had accused her mother of moving the statue forward on purpose to have it fall, and she was giving some angry retort, the door-bell rung, and before orders of "not at home" could be given, the man, who with the cook, had both come upon the scene of action, opened the door, and in walked Mr. George Alexander Waltringham.

There is an old saying, that oil poured upon

a raging sea, will calm the turbulent waters. Perhaps it was owing to the oily nature of the gentleman, that he produced the same effect upon the turbulence of the waves that were raging but a moment before in this family.

The new comer was not at all disconcerted; in fact he was rather inclined to joke at the accident, which he did not look upon as very serious,—in fact he had rather expected it; as he had noticed the insecurity of the thing, which a slight jar might bring down. He forgot to add that he had purposely moved it forward with that view, looking upon it as he did, as such an abortion that it was no harm to work its destruction.

It is but right to do him the justice to say, that he did not anticipate the other damage—the table had been placed under the niche subsequently, by somebody, or rather "nobody," that omnipresent genius of mischief, who was constantly putting things out of place in this house.

The party left the servants to clear away the debris, and retired to the parlor in such a pleasant mood of lively conversation, that

Salinda could only compare it to the sudden outburst of the sun from dark clouds that a moment before had shot forth forked lightning.

In handling some of the things, Salinda discovered that she had soiled her hands, and whispered Kitty to go up to her room with her, where she could wash them. It was an unadvised admission behind the scenes of outside appearances.

"Such a room," she said to Lillie that night in their own neat apartment, "I never saw before—I hope never to see again. The bed looked like a pig's nest; I am sure it had not been made for a week, and the sheets and pillow-cases were fairly black. Every vessel was full of dirty slops, and the only way that I could wash my hands was by Kitty pouring water out of a broken pitcher, while I held them over a flower-pot that seemed grateful for the accidental watering. The whole room looked like the drift of an inundation of some muddy river. Shoes and shifts; books and bonnets; parasols and petticoats; stockings and staylace; tape and towels; slippers and slops; lay about in one grand mixture. The furniture had been costly, if not rich; now there was not a whole chair among half a dozen, and all were loaded with dresses, or some of the paraphernalia of a lady's dressing chamber. The rosewood dressing table stood upon three legs; the sofa seat was broken down in the springs, and the feet had lost the castors, and torn the Turkey carpet. The lace window-curtains were yellow, and covered with dust and cobwebs. But that was no worse than the parlor. Did you notice the festoons the spiders had made all along the cornice over the window?"

"Yes, and the dust among the untouched books on the centre table. It would make my mother crazy."

As Salinda returned to the parlor, there was a commotion in the tea-room. Ned was ordering the cook, with a few of his young gentleman oaths, to give him something from the table to eat, before the company came in. She heard him say: "I will have some—they'll eat it all up—I'm hungry—I won't wait—I'll steal it all, and tell my mother that you eat it, and make her discharge you, if you don't give me some, you blasted old"—

The balance of the sentence was interrupted by a scream from the cook. It was a custard in an elegant cut-glass dish that the boys coveted. Bread, and butter, and cake would not satisfy them. Cook had set the dish on the top shelf of the china closet, to keep it out of their way. While Ned was trying to coax or scold the cook into gratifying his appetite, his brother, the mad bull, like his prototype in a crockery store, had got into the china closet, and climbed up the shelves, and got his hand on the coveted article. It is almost needless to say, that just as he sang out, "Hurrah, Ned, I've got it," he did get it. His foot slipped, and down he came, dish and all, with the contents in his face and all over his clothes, and the dish in fragments on the floor.

"I do wonder," said Mrs. Doolittle, "what that careless wench has broken now. I shall take it out of her wages, she may rest assured of that."

To prevent any one else going to see, she said, "sit still, don't mind it; you know one broken dish always has another just behind it, till fate gets the three."

Kitty lacked the discreetness of her mother and sister. She had turned off as she came down stairs, "to see what the muss was;" and now came in and told the whole story. Her mother was sure it was all the cook's fault.

"She is always having a difficulty with them boys. I dare say if she had given them anything in the world to eat, they would have gone away as quiet as lambs to their play. I declare I must get a new woman—I can't stand it."

What good would it do to get a new one? She had done the same thing a dozen times, with the same results. If she could have got a new system of family government, and brought her children under a wholesome discipline, and taught them subordination, she would have saved herself from constant scenes of vexation and loss, and then the Doolittle boys would not have been the terror of their schoolmates, and the hated pests of the whole neighborhood.

In spite of all the mishaps, tea was at

length ready. How unlike the quiet tea-table of the Saverys; how different from that pleasant, simple meal at the farm. The table was loaded with cut-glass and china, costly and fragile. But the sweet home-made bread and plain cakes were not there. Their place was occupied by costly knick-knackeries from the French baker's—real health-destroyers. The tea was the only home-made thing, and that was weak and smoky, and when it was too late to remedy the defect, it was found that "nobody" had drank up all the milk. Mrs. Doolittle said, "she would warrant it was John, the great hog."

Lillie did not say she would warrant it was not; but from where she sat, she could see the face of a boy peeping into the window through the grape-vine, upon whose lips the stolen milk had left its mark.

It was a costly, but an unsatisfactory meal. The cakes looked as though they were made for ornament and not use, and so they were generally refused. It was not the first time they had done service in the same way. The rich sweetmeats were not half as good or as healthy as Mrs. Whitlock's strawberries. The stiff attempts at gentility were not half as pleasing as the plain conversation and hearty manifest welcome of that meal, which constantly intruded itself in contrast with this. There each lingered, loth to part. Here visitors and visited felt relieved from a tiresome restraint when the good-bye, and hollow-hearted "do come again," had been said. At least one party was wiser, if not happier.

"I have learned," said Salinda, "a lesson for life. I trust I shall never forget to profit by it, if I should ever be a mother."

"I do not think," said Mrs. Savery, "that it is necessary for you or Lillie to wait that event, to apply the lesson of the day to a good purpose. You see the effect of insubordination, and the cost of not training up a child in the way he should go."

"It is certainly very bad economy; besides being extremely vexatious; but Mrs. Doolittle appears to be used to it; don't you think, Mrs. Savery, that she stands it remarkably well? How calm she remained through all the storm."

"Only to storm herself as soon as our backs are turned, and she is free from restraint."

CHAPTER VII.

Family Scenes, and Home Influences.

You that are strong in good purposes, shall not censure the want of strength in Doolittle, to enter upon such a scene as was enacting when he came home—one oft enacted, yet, like all evil acts, growing stronger, growing worse and worse every day.

He hesitated with his hand upon the latch; he heard his wife say that she would "make their father tie them up, and she would whip them to death."

He supposed it was the girls that she meant, for she was talking with them, and he thought; "What, has it come to this? must I tie up my daughters, for their mother to wreak her vengeance upon, for some trifling dispute or disagreement? Never!" Yet he knew full well that her will was law, and if she willed it, he must obey, or have a fight himself.

What should he do? What did he do? Just what a thousand others have before, whose home held no magnet, like that of the Saverys, to draw them within its portals, and shield them from the corrupting association of evil companions.

Poor Doolittle! He had come home late and tired, because it had been hinted to him that his presence with company would not be agreeable.

Such a man trembles as he lays his hand upon his own door-latch, after a hard day's work, and shrinks back from what he hears within. He hesitated, and mentally said, "Oh, God, is this *home?*" then turned away and walked back around the corner, and entered one of those ever invitingly open doors, where a man whose face is one constant winning smile, stood before his customers, tempting them to buy some of his colored fluids, which they knew by experience would give them oblivion of the discomforts of their home, or make them forgetful of their own folly, or reckless of some indiscretion committed or contemplated, or careless of the want of money to provide home comforts, which in such places as this are foolishly wasted.

Doolittle needed no coaxing. He took the draught eagerly, and it was a large one, and then went and sat down in a dark corner and laid his head upon a table and enjoyed —— yes, that is the word, enjoyed the oblivion produced by a drunken sleep. He had long been a hard drinking man, but this was the first time that he had ever been drunk,—drunk in a public bar-room.

He slept on unnoticed, as had a hundred others before him in the same corner. It is the effect, the least injurious effect, of drinking, upon some men. Some are loquacious; some are argumentative and religious; some are lascivious; some are excessively foolish; some are brutal, beastly, ugly, quarrelsome, wicked, combatative, murderous. Others are simply stupid. That was the effect produced upon Doolittle. He waked at length, as many persons have awaked from a state of insensibility, by the sound of their own name.

Close by where he sat, was a thin board partition. Somebody on the other side had forgotten that walls have ears. If they had not, Doolittle had, and when he heard his own name he opened them. His stupor had passed off, and his hearing faculties were quick. He distinguished one of the voices as that of Waltringham. The other he did not know, but the person was pressing him for a debt, which in the fashionable parlance of perverted language, is called "a debt of honor." If it is, it is honor among thieves, for gambling and stealing are both in one category, in the opinion of those who practice neither.

"Now, see here," said Waltringham to his companion, "you just keep easy a little while, and I shall make a raise. See if I don't. I understand the ropes. I am just now stocking the cards. I shall be sure to hold a hand that will win."

"Well, old fellow, I should like to know how. Show me your hand. Is it all honors?"

"Yes, trumps at that. The bullet, king, queen and knave."

There could be no mistake about the latter. Every inch a knave.

"Well, how are you going to play them?

If it is a winning game, I'll take a hand, hold stakes, or count my fingers for you, and come in for a share. What say?"

"Just the thing. I'll tell you. But let us see that we are all alone. Shut that door will you. Is the coast clear?"

'There is nobody in the bar-room except one poor drunken ass, hard and fast in sleepy corner. Go ahead."

Doolittle ventured to look up. He had out-slept all the company. It was after eleven o'clock. The bar-keeper was dozing outside the door, waiting for twelve o'clock, when he would shut up. Doolittle drew up still closer to the partition. There was a large knot hole, covered by a piece of paper, just by his ear. He cut this away with his pocket knife and every low spoken word came through distinctly.

"You know old Doolittle, said Waltringham —very well, his daughter is just one of the finest animals you ever saw trotted out. She is a real 2. 40 nag. She will win anywhere. She will carry me in where the gate would be shut and locked without her. I tell you, she can let down the bars that lead to pleasant pasture. She will last good for years, and then bring cost. Well, that nag is mine. The old woman says that; and the grey mare is the best horse there, I tell you."

"But that don't bring the money. Besides, it will cost a pile to keep such a blooded animal."

"Oh, never fear that. The old man has got plenty of fodder, if he has not plenty of money. I mean to live off of him."

"Very fine for you, but I don't see how that is to get me my money."

"Hold easy. You haven't heard half of it yet. This is game that can't all be bagged at once. The old woman is a fool. I can wind her round my finger. I persuaded her and the girls to make the old man buy a carriage and pair, just to cut a figure. He loves his toddy, and is always good-natured when he is drinking, and as soon as we are married, I will make a raise out of him, through the old woman and girls; you had better believe I will."

"How are you going to do that?"

"Now, I am coming to your share. I must have a partner. I will propose to go into business; that will tickle the old woman to have her son-in-law a merchant. I will offer to take Doolittle in as third partner. His credit is good, and notes signed by you and me, endorsed by him will buy goods. We will ship them and then ship ourselves. But first, you must buy that carriage and horses, which I can persuade them to sell, when I take the daughter off. That will pay your debt, and I will take the goods and the girl for my share. How do you like it?"

"Why, it looks fair. When will you bring it round? I'm in a hurry. To tell you the truth, I am confounded hard up, and must make a raise soon, or I shall have to cut stick."

"I'll settle the matter to-morrow, if I find the old man in the right tune. He must have just so much rum aboard to make things go easy. If he gets too much he goes to sleep, and will snooze away all the evening like a fat pig. I meant to have arranged matters to-day, but the cards had a bad run. The boys, who are as ungoverned as grizzly bears, got into a fight and broke about fifty dollars worth of stuff, and put the old woman in a bad humor. Then they had some stiff, vinegar-faced puritans there to tea, that cut off all conversation. I had to measure my words."

"I tell you what it is, Alleck, this looks like a scurvy trick; but necessity knows no law; and if it wa'n't for fear my wife would turn up and get me in limbo, I would marry the other girl. You say she is fresh?"

"Smooth as a three-year old. Come, go in to win. I will introduce you as a Southern merchant here buying goods, and then you in your generosity shall offer me a partnership, and I will agree to go in, if Doólittle will take a hand. He will say he cannot raise the money, and then I will bring about the horse-trade. Depend upon it, we can skin that drunken fool before he knows it."

"Skin a drunken fool, and that fool is me," said Doolittle to himself. "I have heard enough; I have sat for my portrait, and it has been drawn by an artist. It is a fallacy that listeners never hear any good of themselves. I have heard that which will do me good. I have heard what is rarely spoken of a man to his face—the truth—and I mean to profit by it."

By the time he had finished his colloquy, he once more had his hand upon his own door-latch. He entered with a different feeling from that of the early evening, but it was not a happy one. All was silent, as before all had been stormy. The storm had spent itself. There was a desolateness in the house, but a greater one in his heart. He was sober now, but he felt the guilt of drunkenness as he had never felt it before, and as he then felt, never would feel it again. Mrs. Doolittle was in bed; asleep or pretending to be. She had retired completely worn down in body and mind. She had scolded and fumed at the girls; quarrelled with John and the cook, till both had told her they would leave in the morning, which she had averted by promising an increase of wages. With the boys she had had a regular pitched battle—it was not doubtful which had won the field.

It was a scene that always has the same termination—the parent yields to the child, and that is the end of parental control, and the wretched rule of insubordination. The young tyrant locked his mother in the garden, and then required all sorts of promises before he would open the door, and finally would only agree to throw the key down, and that Ned alone should come in the chamber that night. He plainly told his mother that he did not believe her, and would not trust her word —"you have broken it so often."

Mothers, let this be a lesson. Never give a child reason to say, "you have broken your word." Establish family discipline, and steadily maintain it. Train up a child in the way he should go, from the cradle, and you never will have to chase him down like a wild animal when he merits punishment, nor sue to him to unlock the door and let you into your own house.

Mrs. Doolittle went to her bed, if not a wiser and a better woman, a very dissatisfied and tired one. It is no wonder, if she was not asleep, that she had no further disposition to quarrel, and that she was willing to let her husband lay down in quiet, without making him give an account of himself, and where he had been, and what he had been about till twelve o'clock at night. Her rage and disappointment had overcome her, and worn her down worse than a week of such "slavish labor," as she was in the habit of saying Mrs. Savery inflicted upon herself. If she did, she did not inflict upon herself such a bitter, wretched, sleepless night, as this one that now tormented, instead of refreshed Mrs. Doolittle. Had she known all that her husband knew, she would have been still more wretched; for the marriage of Triphenia with a Southern planter was to be to her a crowning glory.

The girls had gone off to their room; that room so graphically described by Salinda; and there they were having a pretty quarrel between themselves.

Triphenia was mad because Kitty had brought Salinda up there to see all the dirt and confusion, and waste, and discomfort of such an apartment.

It ended in both criminating each other for what they were both guilty of—sloth and indolence. It finally grew so warm, that Triphenia declared that she would not sleep there—she would not sleep in the house—never would sleep there again. In this she kept her word, though she did not probably intend it. She left the house in anger five minutes before her father came in.

The "scene" that Doolittle took a part in the next morning, was not "first exhibited in that theatre for the only time." It was a family scene, but such as never occurs in "well regulated families."

We will not try to peep behind the curtain, for fear,

> "Some power the gift would gie us
> To see ourselves as others see us."

He was miserable, wretched beyond conception. Yesterday, he would have applied a panacea. To day, he would die sooner than touch a drop. He was a stubborn man, and having once made up his mind to a thing would not back out for trifles. He could even withstand the urging of his wife, when she had got over her first blast, "to take a little something; do now, dear, you will feel better."

Strange is it not, that a wife should urge a husband to be a "drunken fool."

Triphenia almost boiled with rage when she heard her father's story; not that she had thrown her love away upon such a worthless fellow, but that his true character had been found out, and that he stood like a convicted felon, to be despised by all honest men. She was still more angry to think she was detected in such a web of falsehoods as she had been weaving. But she concluded, instead of repenting and asking forgiveness, to play the heroic. She declared it was all a conspiracy to prevent her marriage, but it came too late. She did not ask any favors of her father—particularly of such a father."

"Then you can take your 'gentleman' and leave your father and his house as soon as you please. You are no longer a daughter of mine."

Mr. Doolittle hurried away, and shortly afterwards Triphenia left in a rage, declaring she never would again cross the threshold of her father's house.

It was only another lesson in the evils of insubordination.

"I am really glad to hear how much more amiable of the two Kitty has proved herself," said Mrs. Savery, when she heard the story.

"Yes, mother," said Lillie, "for instead of opposing her, she did all she could to help her sister. Her mother got down on her knees and begged Triphenia to stay; declaring that her father should acknowledge his fault and beg her pardon for his brutal treatment, and receive Mr. Waltringham into the family, and then they would all live there so happy together. But she would not listen, but ordered John to bring out the carriage, and took her trunks, and bandboxes, and drove off, leaving her mother without a parting word, and returning Kitty's good wishes with an angry toss of her head. Of course the family are in distress this evening; nobody knows where Triphenia or Mr. Doolittle are, but folks guess that he is ——

"Drunk. I will give you the word, since you hesitate to speak it. But you may rest easy about that. Look here."

Mr. Savery took from his pocket a very neatly engraved card with Mr. Doolittle's name written in bold characters at the bottom.

"I am going to put this in a handsome frame, and then he will hang it up in his bed room. This is a temperance pledge; and it will be kept too, for it is made by a sober man, in good faith, with his eyes fully opened to the folly of his past career. I know where the lost man has been all day. He came directly from his house to my shop. He was so agitated at first that he could not speak; he took me by the hand and led me into my little office-room, and sat down and wiped away the great drops of sweat, and with them some other drops that came from the eyes, and then said:

"'To convince you that I am in earnest, first give me one of those temperance pledges that I have so often rejected.' He wrote his name as you see it there, and put his hand upon his heart, and repeated every word, and said, 'With God's help this will I faithfully keep.' 'Amen,' said I.

"'And now,' said he, 'I want to sign

something else. Jotham Savery, I am ruined. I don't own a dollar's worth of property in the world. It all belongs to my creditors, and I want to make an assignment for their mutual benefit, so that all may get a fair share. If not sacrificed, there may be enough to pay all. My workmen must be paid first in full. It is their due, for they have families dependent upon their wages. My stock must be paid for next. Then the grocer, and butcher, and provision man, and lastly the furniture dealers, unless they will take back so much of their costly gingerbread work as remains uninjured. If so, let them have it at twenty per cent. discount. That is just, and that is what I desire to be in all this transaction. The debt for that foolish purchase of carriage and horses must take its chance—it is not worthy of preference—unless the man chooses to take back the property at exactly what I was to pay for it. My family I shall move back to the country to-morrow, and I want you to give them such furniture as they need—nothing more—and the remainder must be sold.

"'If my creditors will let me go on with my

business, I can soon pay all, with my expenses lessened so much. I can go back and forth on the railroad, so that it will be of no consequence to my work that I live out of town, but it will be of a great deal of consequence to my family.'

"'We went to a lawyer to get the documents put into a legal form. The lawyer knew me very well, but he did not know Doolittle, and so went on with his story of a client who was in limbo on a double charge: one for a suspicion of debt—one of those debts of honor—and the other a charge of forgery. "It seems," said he, "that both my client and his antagonist are a couple of precious scoundrels, and that no longer ago than last night they entered into a conspiracy to marry the two daughters of a good-natured sort of a good-for-nothing, drinking fellow, by the name of Doolittle, who has some property, which the villains were to cheat him out of, as well as his daughters. My client had some time ago given his notes to his 'friend' for a gambling debt, which the chap wanted. Well, the agreement was that they were to go snacks in cheating this Doolittle, and so make the money for that debt, as well as enough to flash awhile with their new wives. The debtor was to call on the creditor this morning, to concoct further measures. This he did, and at once began talking about the affair; my man trying all the time, by gesticulation and signs, and so forth, to keep him still, and to make him understand that there was somebody in the other room; but he was too dull to take the hint, but began making his terms about the new arrangement.

"'I say, Walt,' said he, I shall insist upon one thing, before I agree to let you off from this debt, and that is, if I like the oldest of these two fillies best, I shall take my choice. Now, mind, that if the oldest Doolittle girl—what did you call her—Tri—Tri—something, pleases my fancy best, I shall take her, and—'

"'Will you?' said a lady, walking out of the next room, and taking the gentleman a slap side of the head; 'will you? Then learn what sort of a one you will take.'

"It seems she had called just in time to hear this exposition. How the fellows pacified her, I don't know, but these chaps are always full of words, and know how to use soft soap as well as a washerwoman. It was quite a contretemps, wasn't it?"

"'It was,' I replied; 'we are all apt to commit just such by our unguarded tongues. For instance, supposing you had been so unguarded as to tell this story in the presence of that very Doolittle.'

"'Oh, you wouldn't catch me at that. I am——'

"'Caught,' said I, laughing; 'caught, as keen as you are.'

"'My dear sir, what apology, what amends can I offer? What shall I do?'

"'Sit right down,' said Doolittle, accepting his hand so good-naturedly; 'sit right down and attend to our business, and never mind what is past. It isn't the first good thing that I have lately heard of myself; that is, it will be good for me, I hope.'

"It was, after all, a very amusing affair, and I have no doubt will be the means of giving Doolittle a valuable legal friend, because he now takes an interest in him that he would not have felt under ordinary circumstances.

"We soon had the papers ready, and I have already seen a portion of the creditors, all of whom are disposed to let me do just what I think best. Tom Whip has agreed to take the horses and carriage back, and is to send up to-night. He has a customer for them on better terms than the discount he offered or. the note.

"I don't expect to be able to do anything with the furniture-men; as they say the articles have been so badly kept, they are not really worth half price. The hardest part will be to get the family to move back to the old place in the country; but they must do it, for a rock is not more firm than Doolittle. He is already a new man.

"Now that is my budget of news. Have we any more?"

"I think," said Charley Goodman, who had been standing some time back of Mr. Savery's chair, holding his finger on his lip as a signal to the others not to notice him, so as not to break the story; "I think," said he, "that I can make a slight addition to your budget."

"Triphenia called in the course of the day, and Waltringham's landlady told her that he had gone to jail, and added a great many expletives about his character, not at all complimentary to him or Tryphenia, for being deceived by such a villain."

"Poor Triphenia," said Salinda, "how humiliating."

"Not half as humiliating as what followed, for she had to return home—to that home which a few hours before she had left in such a contemptuous manner, there to beg upon her knees to be forgiven, before she could gain admittance, or shelter even for the night. It was a new era in her life to submit to her father, and treat him with becoming respect. It is a new era with him, to command respect or to exercise parental authority. But he has been taking lessons to-day; I heard who his teacher was; I only hope that the good work of reform will continue as it has begun; for truly, Doolittle is not a bad man, and his children are smart enough; they only lack control, and the instillation of a little common sense in the place of frivolity in the girls, and stubbornness and mischief in the boys, who, with proper training would make smart men."

"There is still another humiliation in store for them," said Mr. Savery; "to-morrow the family move to the country, and next day the red flag will wave from their late residence, while the auctioneer cries 'going, going, gone,' over the piano, sofas, carpets, and rose-wood bedsteads. If I can close up his business and experiment of city life, with a loss of not more than two thousand dollars, I think I shall leave him with his hands unencumbered to go to work and retrieve the great mistakes of his life. As for the girls, I have no fear; Triphenia was the most foolish, and I hope her severe lesson will be one of good for life; I have known folly cured by such a shock; it will either produce that effect, or send her headlong down the broad road of destruction. Let us hope for the best, and be charitable.

"Kitty never was so deeply imbued with folly, and I am in hopes that when she gets back to the country, and finds that she must, she will take hold of the domestic duties, and make herself a housekeeper. The boys are both to be sent away to a school that I have recommended, where discipline is the first law, and order the second, and where every boy is taught to clean his own room, make his bed, saw his own wood, kindle his fires, black his boots, and keep himself neat and respectable, besides attending to his studies. That will dispose of them; my great fear is about their mother. Doolittle says he expects to have to carry her by force, if he gets her back to the country; 'but,' says he, 'I will do it, if I have to carry her on a hearse.'"

"Oh, Mr. Savery, you should have rebuked him for that."

"I knew it was a strong expression, and so was the provocation. Come, let us adjourn this tea-table talk, and see if we cannot change the subject to one more profitable than the misfortunes, or errors in life, of our neighbors."

CHAPTER VIII.

Reverse of Fortune with the Doolittles—Going back to the Country—Death and its Consequences—Scenes of Terror and Sorrow—Repentance and Reconciliation—Leaving Home for ever.

THE threat of Doolittle simply meant to imply that he had determined that it was for his interest, and the salvation of his family from ruin, that he should go back to the country, and go he would, and his wife must submit. He never before was a stern man, but a revolution had occurred in his character, such as we sometimes see depicted upon the stage; so sudden, so complete, that the actor seems to be playing another part. Doolittle was not acting a part—his was an original character, which might be acted to advantage, for others to study. The scene that was "got up" for his benefit, when he went home from the business of the day with Savery, can better be imagined than described. Mrs. Doolittle, not being able to find him at the shop after sending there repeatedly, had made up her mind that he was away somewhere drunk, and having thus determined, she was not to be convinced by the palpable evidence of her senses, when he returned in the evening, that he was strictly sober. He suffered her to go on with her invectives, and charges of bringing ruin upon the family by his improvidence and laziness, thinking perhaps that the best way was, when the flood-gates were opened, to allow the current to flow until the pond should run out. This may be good policy where the stream comes from a small head, but quite the contrary where it flows from such an exhaustless source as that which supplies the cataract of Niagara.

"A pretty piece of work your drinking and ill temper have made—your drunkenness and your violence have undoubtedly broken off a very desirable match for your daughter—for I don't believe a word of the story you trumped up this morning—it was only a drunken dream, or else sheer spite against that lovely young man—you never liked him, you know you didn't, and you need not deny it."

"I am not at all disposed to: I own it: and am proud to think that my intellect was not so obfusticated that I could not properly judge his character."

"Do hear the man—was anything ever like it—one to hear you talk would think he was an imposter, or perhaps some escaped convict."

"He may have been, but he will not escape now—he is in limbo for forgery, and I don't know how many other crimes, and will not be likely to get clear unless he breaks jail."

"Breaks jail! Is he in jail? He is! and you stand there talking about it so coolly. If he is in jail, where is your daughter—where is Triphenia—what is to become of her—Oh you monster, thus to break up your family. I should not wonder if you were the death of poor Triphenia. In the frame of mind she was in when she left home this morning, I should not be surprised if she committed suicide: and all through the conduct of her father. There," as she heard the door bell ring, "do run, Kitty, and see if it is not some messenger from the poor girl, or else to tell us that she has gone where no message will ever come from her to her poor distracted mother."

Kitty was absent so long that it was evident that the messenger was not one that brought news of death or any other terrible calamity, though it was one that told of ruined hopes and blasted ambition--that the wild day-dreams of a romantic girl had all been crushed, and herself humbled at a single blow.

It was not a messenger from Triphenia, it was Triphenia herself; humbled, broken down, subdued, and weeping like a child. In one hour the whole of her life had been reviewed, and her errors had rushed back upon her heart, and, like her father, for in many cases she was like him, she had seen what were her errors, and had determined to begin a new course of life. She fell upon Kitty's neck as she opened the door, and then for the first time during all the agony of the twenty-four hours, since the commencement of the quarrel, her fountains of tears were unlocked, and poured forth their streams, greatly to the relief of a heart that until then seemed on fire. As soon as she could speak, she begged Kitty to hide her from her angry father—her mother she knew would storm awhile, but for that she cared nothing; her father "if sober," she said, she could never meet him—she had injured him too deeply to hope for forgiveness. Oh! sister, since you forgive me, hide me, at least for to-night, and don't let any one know that I am here."

To this Kitty acceded, and while Triphenia went quietly up to their room, she went back to tell her mother that she had heard from her sister, and that she was in a friend's house safe and well, and that her mother should see her in the morning. She then drew her father away, as she said, to give him some supper, but in reality to pave the way for a reconciliation with Triphenia.

Doolittle was a man of a kind disposition, and loved his children, and loved their caresses, and therefore said yes, without an effort, when Kitty put her arms around his neck and said, "father, you will forgive her?" Her heart leapt with joy to hear that little word, "yes."

"Oh come then, now, for she is so miserable"—and she took him by the arm, without regarding his question "where?" and led him up to her chamber.

That "there is a time for all things," was partly proved by the fact that there is a time for penitence. Then was the time for Triphenia. She fell upon her father's neck, a subdued, penitent child. All the errors of her former conduct seemed to have concentrated upon her mind, and to be brought by the one great error of her stubborn temper to a culminating point, and from that she had resolved that change, improvement, and something better should arise. In this she was greatly assisted by her father's ready forgiveness of her fault, but still more from the fact that he had determined never to touch another drop of intoxicating liquor.

"In this," said he, "my girls, I need all my own strength, and all that you can lend me. I have another severe trial for you, and to accomplish it in peace I shall also need your aid. I am utterly ruined in business, and have made an assignment, for the benefit of my creditors, of all my property, this house and furniture included, except the few plain things that we shall need in the country, where we are to go to-morrow; and I want your assistance to reconcile your mother, who has so often declared that she never will go back alive; and, I am sorry to say, she has been sustained by her daughters, against the convictions of their father."

"But shall not be any more. If you have been unfortunate, and find it best to return to the old place, you never shall say again that we were stubborn and prevented it, and I hope mother will be reasonable. Have you told her?"

"Not yet; but I will, now that I have got somebody to help me. Shall I do it to-night?"

"Yes, now; the sooner the better; let's have it over with. Don't you say so, sister?"

"Certainly; and then we shall be better prepared for our task to-morrow."

Poor girls, they little knew what that task was to be. Although *now* is generally the best time, it was not so in this case. Mrs. Doolittle, with all her scolding of her husband for drinking, was not herself entirely free from that foolish vice. Besides, she had been all day in a state of intense nervous excitement, which was aggravated by several potations, taken as certain antidotes for her disease.

"It would have been better to have waited until morning, before breaking the news to her;" that is, so said they all, after the result was known. Who knows? Better say, all is for the best, however inscrutable. "I want," said Doolittle, "to have a little talk with you about moving to the country."

"Well, I don't want to hear anything about it. I have told you often enough never to speak to me again on the subject. When I am dead you may carry me, not before; I tell you that, once for all, and let that be the end of it."

"But it can't be the end of it; we have got to move from here; this house and furniture has got to be sold to pay my debts. I have failed."

"I know you have; you have been failing ever since I knew you. If you have drank up this house, it is no more than I expected; but

I can tell you, nobody is going to get me out alive. I am not going to take my girls back to the country, after I have spent so much to give them a genteel city education, and have got a fashionably furnished house for them to live in: depend upon that. If you choose to go, you may go, and the girls and I—"

"The girls have already agreed to go, so it will be you who will have to stay alone."

"It is a lie; it is no such thing; my girls—"

"Have both agreed to go with father, and have come to urge you to consent to go with us freely."

"Freely! freely! ha! go freely! then I am to be coerced if I don't go freely, am I? Hold your tongue—you are a pretty baggage—how that word grated upon Triphenia's ear—to join your father in a conspiracy against me. No, I won't go, I tell you all, to save you from falling dead at my feet. I—I—I—Oh, God forgive me!—husband!—Kitty!—Tri———e—e—Oh!"

Mrs. Doolittle was ready to go; the period had arrived when she would make no further opposition. As she was uttering the words, "falling dead at my feet," she had risen from her chair, and stretched out her hands in a menacing manner towards the girls, upon whom her anger seemed to fall most bitter, for having, as she thought, deserted her, and gone over to her husband's side. For a moment she looked wildly terrible; so much so that they were afraid to approach her. Mr. Doolittle had seen so many of her hysteric fits that he was not alarmed, until her voice changed to that of prayer, and then he hardly knew whether it was penitence or anger, until she called him and the girls by name, and in trying to finish Triphenia's name, turned black in the face with suffocation, and before he could spring across the room to catch her, she pitched forward toward his outstretched arms, and fell heavily upon the carpet, a corpse.

The time had come, Oh, how soon! "When I am dead you may carry me." He carried her first to a sofa, and others rushed out for a surgeon. First one, then two, three, for notwithstanding it was midnight, the news spread, and each one that heard it ran for another doctor. It was of no use. The first one pronounced her dead—dead from suffocation—a very common effect upon obese persons of violent temper, resulting from sudden anger.

CHAPTER IX.

Six Months on Time's Railroad—Talk of Marriage--Sensible Conclusion to get ready first—Preparation for House-keeping—The New House—A Pleasant Surprise.

How rapidly six months went down the inclined plane of Time's railroad, carrying along the daily trains of cars freighted with hopes, anticipations, prospects of things to happen before the train reaches the final termination; and how anxiously had those waiting at the roadside stations, watched each day for the one that would bring the culmination of the hope nearest the heart.

Charley Goodman was among those watching and waiting. Yet he was not impatient, for reason told him that in no six months of Salinda's life, had she travelled so fast upon the road of improvement that lifts the civilized, cultivated, educated woman, above one bred in savage life, or reared in health-destroying indolence of families who suppose themselves the very acme of Christian civilization.

"Six months," said he to her one evening, "of my probation have passed. It is the first period that you set—'six months or a year'—those were the words; do you intend to keep me waiting for the longest period?"

"Why, Charley, the time has gone so rapidly, that I can hardly realize that so many months of my life have been sped away never to return. But there is a lesson in that, well worthy of thought—careful, serious thought—it should teach us the economy of time. To look back, I cannot see where I have wasted mine, but to look forward it seems as though I should be able to accomplish a great deal more in the next six months than I have in the past. I do hope they will be as happy ones to me as the past have been. And one of the most happy of all the circumstances connected with them, is, that I am so much better fitted to be your wife than I was before."

"Then when will you be that coveted object?"

"You remember the promise—'six months or a year'—I shall leave it to you to decide, after I state a few circumstances. Neither of us having previously determined upon our marriage at this time, neither are prepared; and I have not been six months studying economy, without learning what a waste of time it would be to get married before we are prepared. Some romance reading young girls, seem to think that it would be the very perfection of cunning mystery, to get married so suddenly or so slyly, that none of their friends would know of the courtship, until they were introduced as Mrs. Jones or Mrs. Smith. But that is not the case with us—it is well known that we are affianced—we make no mystery of our intention to get married—when we get ready—and that is what I propose now to do; and that will be carrying out the principles of economy that I have learned in this house. It is now the beginning of winter: the year will end in May, that sweetest of all the months of the year for a bright honey-moon; and during the winter I will devote my leisure time to looking up, buying, making, and getting together all the little et ceteras of house-keeping; in doing which I shall find the advice of Mrs. Savery and the assistance of Lillie almost invaluable. In the meantime you shall determine where we are to live, and get our house ready, and next May-day we will move into it in the morning, and at dinner time you shall have your first meal provided by the hands of your own dear wife. Now, is not that a lesson of economy, worth all the romantic marriages of Gretna Green?"

"You are a blessed angel, and you shall be my guide, I hope, through a long life of happiness."

"Rather, we will go hand-in-hand, my voice cheering you, and your strength sustaining me. It is thus a man and wife should live, and then they will be happy."

It was very true, as Salinda said, that the advice of Mrs. Savery would prove invaluable in providing for house-keeping. Her father was willing to purchase almost any amount of costly furniture, but Salinda steadily refused. She wanted first to see where it was to be put, and then she would determine what she would have.

"That you shall see to-morrow morning," said Charley. It was now winter, but one of those clear, mild days that make an American winter so delightful, when Salinda went to see the spot selected for her future home. She was aware that something had been going on for some time between Mr. Savery and Charley, which they were not disposed to let her into the secret of; but whether it was a house or some article of furniture, she was not certain. However, this clear, beautiful morning was to determine the extent of their secrets. Just on the outskirts of the town lived old Captain Peabody, whose wife kept the cow that eat the grass saved by Frank from the garden borders and grass plot. Salinda had often admired the place, it was so neat, with its large garden and fruit trees, and little white stable, and old well, and green grass, and shady yard; but the old house, like its old occupants, had been in its prime fifty years ago. Both had seen their day, and the old lady had gone to her last home, leaving her old partner the sole occupant of their late one—now home no more; and he had been persuaded to part with it, and go and spend the remainder of his days with a daughter in the country. It was a sad thing to go and leave a house where he had lived over fifty years, and all the choice trees and shrubs that bore fruit and flowers; but it was a consolation to the old man to know into whose hands all his treasured things were going to fall, and that the place would be occupied by those who would not only permit, but welcome his occasional visits.

"If it warn't for the poor old house looking so shabby," said Capt. Peabody to Charley Goodman, "I would offer to sell you my place, because your Salinda would so appreciate the garden and fruit, and all the little conveniences that make life comfortable; and I would sell it to you cheaper than to any other person I know of, because I know that I should always meet with such a kind welcome and sweet smile from her; when I came to look after my pet trees, and, perhaps, use my pruning knife here and there as it was needed. I really must stipulate for the privilege of trimming the grape vines every season, as I could not bear to see them grow worthless for want of care. Ah! it is not many years that I shall care for them at best."

"No matter for the shabbiness of the house;

you know I am a carpenter, and can soon fix that; if you have a mind to sell me the place, you shall retain your old bed room, and always find it in order whenever you will come down and spend a night or a week or month in your old home. I shall think it good economy to make such an arrangement, for the many things that you can teach me, not only in pruning the vines, but in everything else, by which you have kept the place in such order that it attracts the attention of all passing by; and as for Salinda, you know how much she loves a garden and shrubbery."

"And shall have it. I don't want the money, but I suppose it is worth a thousand dollars, perhaps it would sell for more, but no matter; I want that sum secured to my four grandchildren, when they come of age, and the place is yours; is it a bargain?"

"It is; I will have the papers prepared to-morrow, and go to work at once, and you shall soon see how quick I can cure the house of its shabby appearance. If you please, do not tell Salinda; I want to give her a pleasant little surprise."

He did so upon the morning mentioned. The place was about a mile from Mr. Savery's, and the day clear, dry and bracing. He offered to get a carriage, but she simply said, "would that be good economy?" It would not, because the walk was not only pleasant, but in such air, particularly healthy. It would be good economy for ladies to take many such walks.

The plan arranged was, that Mrs. Savery and the girls should start whenever they got ready, and Mr. Savery and Charley would meet them at the Capt. Peabody place, where, it was understood, they were at work fixing up the house for sale, and go from there to the house he talked of occupying, which was close by, in that pleasant neighborhood.

"Dear me, Mrs. Savery," said Salinda, "do look what a pretty cottage they have made where the old house used to stand. I declare I wish Charley could have bought that, it would have been perfectly lovely. Who did he say was going to live there? I am afraid that I shall break the tenth commandment."

"I hope not; I do not recollect that he ever

told me who was going to live here, but whoever it is will have a very pleasant home; the old man has a valuable collection of fruit."

"Whoever has it, I hope will give him a share while he lives; I am sure he is entitled to it over and above all the money price."

"That is a good sentiment, Salinda; let us step in and inquire who the new owner is, and whether he will be likely to carry out your wishes."

They found, upon examination, that the old house had not been taken away entirely; it was only remodeled. The frame was one of the old sort of solid oak, calculated to endure for ever, upon its firm stone-wall foundation, that extended to the bottom of a dry cellar, and there rested upon a rock. Upon such a foundation a more modern form had been wrought out of the old fabric. The large stone chimney had been removed from the center, and two brick tops added to the roof, which had been changed into a gothic form, and tops are only needed where stoves take the place of hearth-stones. In the place of the chimney was now a stair-way to four good bed-rooms above, and to cellar, milk-room, and coal-room below.

The space formerly occupied by the stairway was now included in a hall; so that, instead of a cramped, narrow entry, there was a fine, roomy space, which would often be used for a sitting-room in summer. The parlor was the same old square room, the white ash floor of which had never known a carpet; but how changed its appearance; for in place of the great stone fire-place stood a bright coal stove, and the little windows of small panes of glass had given way to a large projecting window upon each—the north and east—side, reaching from floor to ceiling, which, with the walls, had been papered upon the half century old plastering.

The "common room" had undergone another metamorphosis; for the back windows were hidden by a new building for a kitchen, store-room and pantries, the latter of which formerly occupied the east end of this room, but had been removed, and the room carried out six feet, with long windows opening on the north, south and east sides, making a pleasant alcove both summer and winter, looking out upon the grass-plot and flower-garden, and within reach of two plum trees and a nectarine.

At the other end of this room was a bed-room—it was the one that this good couple had slept in for fifty years, and it looked as though it might have been occupied up to this moment by the same persons without change. It was the only thing unchanged about the house. Salinda expressed her surprise. She was delighted with every thing she saw, and admired the taste of the new purchaser in all his alterations; but this room was a phenomenon, and she exclaimed, "What does it mean?"

"It is the intention of the old captain to pay the new occupant an occasional visit, to look after his favorite fruit trees, and prune and keep them in bearing—"

"And to eat the fruit, I hope."

"Yes, I hope so, for many years; and the purchaser has thought how pleasant it would be for the old man at such times to occupy his old room, just as he did when the place was all his own. It will be pleasant, too, I hope to the new owners."

"Yes, and grateful in the sight of Heaven, to see such kind consideration for the aged, the poor bereaved old man. How it must ease the pang with which he parted with his home. Oh! I could hug the purchaser to my heart for this," said Salinda, with enthusiasm.

"Then do it," said Charley, bursting into a joyous laugh, in which he was joined by the others, while he folded the astonished, but thrice happy girl, in his arms. Happy to think this lovely home was hers—happy to think the praise of this noble act which she had so applauded, was due to the man she had chosen for a husband—happy to think with what care and pleasure she, with her own hands, would keep that room always in order, while the old man would teach her the names, and how to tend and cultivate the various trees and plants of the garden. As the children sometimes say, she was "happy all over."

"You told me," said Charley, "that I should have all winter to get a house ready, and when

I had got it, you could tell what you wanted to furnish it with; I am now ready for your part; I only stipulate that you shall not order any furniture, except carpets and crockery and small articles, until you see me again upon that subject."

"Another surprise, I suppose; but you have nothing in store that can make me any more happy than I am now—I am full—my excess of pleasure is almost childish. Oh! this is such a home; such a lovely pleasant place, that I feel as though I could not be thankful enough. But I will not let my pleasure interfere with my business, if I am to buy the furniture, the first thing is to get the measurement of the rooms for the carpets. Will you give me that, while I make a memorandum, as we go from room to room, with Mrs. Savery's assistance, of the various articles necessary — mind the word, necessary — for I intend to get no others, that we shall require. Lillie, will you act as clerk, you are so quick with a pencil? Here is my memorandum book. Where shall we begin?"

"In the kitchen, certainly," said Mrs.

Savery, "for there, of all other parts of the house, is where things are necessary, yet there is where they are most neglected. In the first place, Lillie, you may make a memorandum of the tin ware from your recollection of what we have at home; and always bear in mind, Salinda, that buying cheap tin ware is throwing money away; none, but the very best double plate, should ever be used, and such will last a life time — the poorest kind will wear out in a year. Upon the same principle, never buy low priced earthen ware, particularly that which looks like the substance of a common brick, when broken. The solid strong stone ware costs, perhaps, a quarter more, and is worth ten times as much as the other.

"The same remark will apply to iron and wooden ware; it is much more economical to buy the best at first. Put down a looking glass, Lillie; every kitchen should have a looking glass, so that whoever has occasion to go from there to the parlor may not be mortified, when she catches a glance in the great mirror, to see that her hair or dress is all awry. A little glass here, that will only cost half a dollar, will save many a dollar's worth of time spent in running up stairs, 'just to fix my hair.'

"You want a good strong oil cloth on the floor; it will save twice its cost in labor before it is worn out. You must have plenty of kitchen towels; if you don't, it is ten chances to one but the first hired girl you have will take a damask table cloth to wipe the dishes, and a fine wiping towel for a pot cloth. The best material in the world, for kitchen cloths, is our country tow linen; it is worth five times as much as the imported crash — trash would be a better name — that almost every body uses."

"What do you advise about carpets?"

"That you buy a substantial three-ply carpet of some only medium dark pattern and cheerful colors, which will in a measure correspond with the furniture, for this room, where you will spend nearly all your time. For the parlor, you may as well get a good Brussels, that will last you a life time, but mind that the pattern is one that has some resemblance to something in the world, and that in both figure and color, it is cheerful. As your stairs are not in a position for show, when the front door is open, I should put down a strip of soft matting, just to break the sounds of the step. You know stair carpeting is going out of fashion and paint is substituted. For your bed-rooms, I would buy a good piece of ingrain, or three-ply, enough to carpet all the rooms alike. Get a pattern of soft colors, a prominent one of which should be green, and the figures, flowers and foliage. As to your bedding, you will find it good economy to get that of good quality throughout. You should have both cotton and linen sheets and pillow cases.

"There, I think that memorandum will last you till next week, and then we will come out again and see how things look, and what Charley has to say about the other furniture."

Next week they did come out again, and sure enough, there was another surprise. Mrs. Lovewell had, unbeknown to Salinda, employed a man to put down the carpets, and Charley had been busy with his part of the plot. He had learned from the Saverys how much of the furniture of a house he could make with his own hands, and while the ordinary work of his trade was slack during the winter, he had thus employed himself, and with the assistance of a painter had succeeded most admirably. Salinda found the four bed-rooms occupied with bedsteads, bureaus, wash-stands, tables and chairs, the cost of which would bear no comparison to the mahogany and rose-wood ones that she was tempted to buy at the Doolittles' sale, because, as the auctioneer said, they went at such a great sacrifice upon first cost.

"Shall I bid?" said Charley to Mr. Savery, when they were selling "so very low."

"No, no; you don't want them—you can make better ones in your own shop with a few boards, a saw, plane, and hammer, and nails, and a little paint."

So he did; and now, here they were. "This," said Mrs. Savery, "is the oak-room—this the maple-room—this the black-walnut room—and this you have so hidden the kind of wood, that we shall have to distinguish it by the color."

"No, we will distinguish it by the ornament; we will call it the tulip-room. The articles are made of the wood of the American tulip-tree, and the painter has very appropriately chosen the flower and leaf for an ornament; just as you see in the oak-room, the handles of the bureau are carved acorns, and oak-leaves, and on the walnut and maple, there is the representation of a leaf in gilt.

"I will add, as they are wanted, more frames for lounges, such as I have in this room and the sitting-room below, where you will find all the necessary tables, benches, etc.; and I would have tried my hand at the parlor furniture, but your mother would not consent. Your father wanted to buy everything, but I said No, and now he is as much delighted as his daughter appears to be; and he declares that he intends to quit business and come and live with us—he has already chosen the oak-room, and says it pleases him better than any imported furniture. You know he is a great tariff man, and goes for home manufactures, and this kind of furnishing just suits his notions. He insisted that all the carpeting should be American."

While Salinda was enjoying her raptures, to see how nice everything looked, and wondering how all these changes would affect the good old man, to whom they owed so much for the embellishments of the ground, which no amount of industry could have given them in the short time it had taken to metamorphose the house, she was startled with the feeling of a hand upon her shoulder—some one had approached unseen, and she turned suddenly, and met the smiling face, glowing beneath the snowy locks of the man she was just talking about in words of such heart-feeling. In another moment—it was impulse without premeditation—a sort of magnetic attraction—he was pressing her in his arms, while she gave him a child-like, affectionate kiss.

"I will tell you what he thinks—how he feels—that in giving up his old home to strangers, he never shall feel like a stranger among them. You will be to me more like a dear child of my own, than a stranger, and all this change does not grieve me half as much as it would to come back to the same old house I left, and find an old hat here, a pillow or old rags there, filling the broken windows, and the whole house occupied with dirt and squalid wretchedness. It is the first time I have seen my old home since I left it—the change is very great, to be sure, but all for the best."

Salinda then took the old man through the house, and showed him the new arrangements and conveniences, with all of which he expressed as much delight as though he had made them himself for a favorite child. At last she opened the door of his old bed-room; and when he saw that amid all the alterations, this had been preserved without change, his heart was too full for utterance. He knew the object, and felt the full force of the kind act; and tears trickled down his cheeks, as he stood offering up a mental prayer for those who showed such feeling for others, that they should never lack ministering angels to their own declining years.

It is strange how little is required to move

the human heart, and since such trifling acts of kindly feeling of one to another produce so much happiness to giver as well as receiver, that we are not more anxious to be kind to one another.

Time now sped on rapidly with the preparations for housekeeping. Few seem to understand the economy, however, of all these preparations before marriage, instead of after; for then the time of the young wife is more or less absorbed by calls of friends, many of which must be returned, or friends and acquaintances will feel that the laws which govern the courtesies of life have been violated.

March, that month of storm, cold and blustering winds, snows and rains, with alternate freezing and thawing, which makes it one of the most uncomfortable months of all the year, had come and gone almost unnoticed by Salinda and the Saverys, so busy were they in this work of preparation. April, too, with its sunshine and showers, its summer hot days, and chilling cold, was rapidly going down the smooth ways that launch the gliding months into eternity, deep-freighted as they are with whatever serves to make up the cargo of joys or sorrows of human life. May-day was now rapidly approaching, and May-day had been set apart by Salinda for that—to a young woman—most important of all days of her life—her wedding-day.

During the winter there had been one subject frequently talked over among those who occupied the sitting-room, and made up that pleasant family circle at the Saverys. That subject was the Doolittle family. The change was indeed a wonderful one. Triphenia had kept her promise to her father to the letter; for she had done all a child could do to make his home a pleasant one, and in this she had been ably assisted by Kitty. Mrs. Savery had been out several times to visit and advise with them, and her instructions were well followed. Triphenia said she was determined to win her approbation as a housekeeper, to as great a degree as she had lost her respect, while absorbed in the folly of trying to ape a class that all her antecedents had unfitted her for. Being naturally of a strong mind, full of the raw material out of which proper education makes a smart, sensible woman, she was quick to learn, and six months' practical education had produced almost as great a change in her, as the same period had in Captain Peabody's old house. Salinda and Lillie had often visited the girls in their humble home in the country, and always came away as much delighted with their visit, as they had been formerly disgusted.

The girls had been persuaded, too, into a new course of reading, and Salinda and Lillie had both undertaken to furnish them books with their own notes and comments, and references to particular chapters, pages or sentences. Charley Goodman, too, had entered into the spirit of the thing, and used to come every spare evening, and while Mrs. Savery and the girls plied their busy needles, he whiled the time away reading aloud; and Mr. Savery, whenever the occasion offered, added some comments, and Frank acted as note-taker, which Lillie afterwards wrote out and sent to the Doolittle girls.

It is perfectly surprising, the amount of information that may be thus treasured up in a family, by this economical use of time in the long winter months.

It should encourage all of us in the prosecution of a good work, when we read what a beneficial influence was wrought upon those wayward girls. Triphenia and Kitty, by these friendly epistles of good advice and encouragement, and the notices of good books, with extracts from their pages, by which a new taste for reading was acquired, and a very vicious habit of reading none but the most exciting novels got rid of, by which both mind and morals were improved.

The last day of April at length arrived. The wedding dress was all ready; it was a simple, plain white muslin; no more expensive than would be appropriate for the daughter of a very humble mechanic. Salinda had steadily rejected all the offers of her parents to provide costly apparel, or jewelry ornaments. "I already have enough," she said, "and I will not grieve a woman who has devoted so much attention to teaching me economy, as Mrs. Savery has, by incurring a useless expenditure." She only asked just enough besides her own simple dress, to apparel her bridesmaid, the dear Lillie, just like herself, and give a new suit to "brother Frank."

Mr. Lovewell had made it "a matter of business" to pay Mrs. Savery punctually every month the sum stipulated for Salinda's "board and tuition." He was always careful to insert these terms in every receipt; and he was just about as careful to send the money on the last day of the month, as he was to pay his notes in bank; and it was always sent in gold. In the excitement of this busy evening, this wonted punctuality had been forgotten by the recipients, but not by the payer of the money, and while they were sitting as usual after tea, in their family chit-chat, a ring was heard upon the door-bell, and while Salinda was wondering if that could be father and mother, the regular monthly messenger was ushered into the room with his "little matter of business."

"I wish," thought Lillie, "that Mr. Precision had for once forgotten that this is the last day of the month, in the evening, and that to-morrow we are going to have a wedding here," for Salinda had stipulated that she might be married in a house that had been to her a home for the happiest year of her life.

Mrs. Savery thought as she took the package and signed the receipt, "I wonder if this punctual man of business formality will let the year pass without ever expressing a single word of approbation, except this regular payment for 'board and tuition'?"

There was nothing to indicate that the man felt that he had any other obligation to discharge, and Mrs. Savery bowed her head upon her hand, it must be owned, slightly sad. She was not a vain woman, but she had that good trait in human nature which prompts many a noble action—a love of approbation. She was so absorbed in thought, that she did not notice that the man, before he left the room, had crossed over and handed a package to Lillie, who was just then wishing the man had not come there. He simply said: "This is for you, Miss Lillie Savery," and bowed himself out of the room.

Lillie sat in a maze of wonder, eyeing the formidable seal which had been affixed by the old clerk with as much scrupulous exactness as though he was going to send it by mail, instead of being his own postman.

"You might as well break it," said her father.

"Break what?" said her mother, for the first time looking up and seeing the astonishment depicted in Lillie's face, as she looked at the package in her hand. Mrs. Savery now wondered. Lillie soon solved the wonder, by clipping the envelope and displaying the contents, the most noticeable of which was a bank stock certificate, made out in the name of Jotham Savery in trust for his daughter Lillie, for one thousand dollars.

There was a short letter addressed to Miss Lillie Savery, begging her to accept the enclosed "as a marriage portion, whenever that event may occur, as a very slight and perfectly inadequate expression of the deep sense of gratitude due you and your family, from your truly sincere friends, Mr. and Mrs. William Lovewell."

Tears trickled down the cheeks of Mrs. Savery, as Lillie read the note, which though very short, was very expressive. Her love of approbation was fully gratified.

It was, perhaps, very well that all minds were just now diverted from this subject by another. Susan said a gentleman was waiting in the passage to speak with Mr. Savery, who went out and said a few words in so low a tone that the voices could not be distinguished, except as he said to the stranger, "Wait till I speak with the girls."

What could he be waiting for? What was to be said to the girls? That was soon known, for Mr. Savery came back with an unusually serious face, and as he entered, said, "Poor Doolittle!"

"Poor Doolittle!" replied Mrs. Savery; "why, you alarm me; what has happened?"

"Nothing has happened yet; but he is likely to lose his housekeeper—that is, his oldest one. Triphenia is going to be married, and like Salinda, she has chosen May-day for her wedding day."

"Then she won't be here—nor Kitty, I suppose. Then who will stand up with Lillie? What a misfortune!"

"I don't know about that; that all depends upon circumstances. She will côme, if you will agree to have a double wedding here, and then all go together out to her husband's home in the country."

"Well, now, in the first place, we should like to know who we are going to entertain, and where we are going to be entertained. Who is the happy man?"

"Really, I never thought to ask his name; but he is in the hall; I will call him in to speak for himself."

He threw open the door, and the gentleman came forward. Lillie was the first to probe the mystery, which he endeavored to keep up by holding his hat before his face. She sprang forward, and had her arms around his neck before he had fairly emerged into the light, uttering a wild exclamation of joy, as she repeated, "Uncle Samuel—uncle Samuel —I thought so: I knew it must be him, for I am sure Triphenia never loved any body else;

and now what a good wife she will make him! But how sly they have been, though!"

If my readers can imagine a more happy wedding party than the one that lunched at the Saverys, and dined at the old Whitlock farm, on the first of May, 185–, or better or more happy wives than those that preside now, at this moment, over Whitlock House and Peabody Cottage, I shall leave them to their imagination.

CHAPTER X.

THE STORY OF A DIME A DAY.

[*Originally printed in The Tribune, Dec. 7, 1855.*]

What shall we Buy?—What one Dime Purchased—A Lesson Learned—What Good can be Done with a Dime—Dying to Live—Starving without Dying—Dimes Wasted—Economy in Fuel—Wasted Fuel—Chips worth Saving—Heat Wasted—Fire Kindlers.

ONE DIME.—'Tis a little sum—'tis often given for a drink or a cigar—'tis soon burned out and wasted. It takes ten dimes to make a dollar, and a dollar is a common price for a single meal. It is soon eaten—its effects are not lasting, except when it produces dyspepsia, and then it often costs a hundred dimes to purchase medicine that does *not* cure the disease.

To those who never dine for less than a dollar, how unsatisfactory would be a dinner for a Dime! Reader, have you ever reflected how many entire families in this city, where food is so dear, dine, every day, for less than one Dime? Did you ever think of bestowing one Dime for charitable purposes, and how much good that would do? What if every subscriber to the *Weekly Tribune* should give one Dime, with his subscription, to be applied to the necessities of the needy, and deserving poor, in this city—did you ever consider what a sum it would be? Look at it—175,000 subscribers, at one Dime each, is $17,500! What if it were applied to purchase bread, say at five cents a loaf! It would buy 3,500,000 loaves of bread. What if we should announce that such a quantity of bread was about to be given to the poor, in this city! The whole land would rejoice. How much can be done with one Dime!

Let us see what we would do with it if we had but one—only one Dime in the world—and yet with that must provide for a family consisting of a mother and four children for a whole day. We would not buy bakers' bread at sixpence a loaf—very small loaves, too, never weighing over a pound, however moist or however adulterated with corn, potatoes, or buckwheat, which are harmless—

or with plaster of Paris, lime, alum, sulphate of zinc, ground bones, and we do not know how many other deleterious substances. No, we would not buy bakers' bread with our Dime, nor would we buy fine flour at six or seven cents a pound, else some of the children would go hungry. We might buy corn meal and make a cheap cake, or a pot of mush, or a larger pot of porridge, or we might buy two pounds of hominy, and then our Dime would feed the family one full meal; but to this latter article there is one objection. Where is the fuel to come from to cook this mess? for corn, more than any other grain, requires cooking to make it palatable and wholesome. Two, three, or even four hours of slow boiling is not too much. Our Dime will not cook as well as buy the corn meal or hominy. What then? Potatoes! Let us see. They require least cooking; but they cost, with all their water—and they are more than half water—two cents and a half a pound at retail.

Then they are not cheap food after all. It will not do to spend our Dime for potatoes.

What then? It is no easy study to learn how to procure the most human food for a Dime; to ascertain how many hungry mouths may be fed—how many empty stomachs satisfied, for one Dime. It is a study too much neglected. It should be taught in all Public Schools. Certainly in all Charity, Industrial, and Ragged Schools, where children are fed as well as taught. What better wisdom could you teach them than how to procure the most food for a Dime? It is a little coin, but can be made to expand. It would be real charity—genuine charity—practical charity—to teach such scholars economy in food; not how to eat less, to live upon less—for Heaven knows some of them live upon little enough now—but to teach them what to buy, in case of emergency, with a little coin—only one Dime. We have lately learned that lesson, and we will teach it to you. We learned it of a woman—that is, the practical operation of it—though she says she learned it of us, from something she read about economizing food, in the *Tribune*.

"I had," said she, "one day last week,

only one Dime in the world, and that was to feed me and my four children all day; for I would not ask for credit, and I would not borrow, and I never did beg. I did live through the day, and I did not go hungry. I fed myself and family with one Dime."

"How?"

"Oh, that was not all. I bought fuel, too."

"What, with one Dime?"

"Yes, with one Dime! I bought two cents' worth of coke, because that is cheaper than coal, and because I could kindle it with a piece of paper in my little furnace, with two or three little bits of charcoal that some careless boy had dropped in the street just in my path. With three cents I bought a scraggy piece of salt pork, half fat and half lean. There might have been half a pound of it—the man did not weigh it. Now half my money was gone, and the show for breakfast, dinner, and supper was certainly a very poor one. With the rest of my Dime I bought four cents' worth of white beans. By-the-by, I got these at night, and soaked them in tepid water on a neighbor's stove till morning. I had one cent left. I bought one cent's worth of corn meal, and the grocery man gave me a red-pepper pod."

"What was that for?"

"Wait a little—you shall know. Of all things, peppers and onions are appreciated by the poor in winter, because they help to keep them warm. With my meal I made three dumplings, and these, with the pork and the pepper-pod, I put into the pot with the beans and plenty of water (for the pork was salt), and boiled the whole two hours; and then we had breakfast, for it was time for the children to go to school. We ate one of the dumplings, and each had a plate of the soup for breakfast, and a very good breakfast it was.

"I kept the pot boiling as long as my coke lasted, and at dinner we ate half the meat, half the soup, and one of the dumplings. We had the same allowance for supper; and the children were better satisfied than I have sometimes seen them when our food has cost five times as much. The next day we had another Dime—it was all I could earn for all

I could get to do—two pairs of men's drawers, each day, at five cents a pair—and on that we lived—lived well. We had a change, too, for instead of the corn meal and beans I got four cents' worth of oat-meal and one cent's worth of potatoes—small potatoes, because I could get more of them. I washed them clean, so as not to waste anything by paring, and cut them up and boiled them all to pieces with the meat and meal."

"Which went furthest?"

"I can't say. We ate it all each day, and did'nt feel the want of more, though the children said: 'Ma, don't you wish we had a piece of bread-and-butter, to finish off with?' It would have been good, to be sure; but, bless me! what would a Dime's worth of bread and butter be for my family? But I had another change next day."

"What, for another Dime?"

"Yes; that was all we had, day after day. We had to live on it. It was very hard, to be sure; but it has taught me something."

"What is that?"

"That poor folks could live a great deal

cheaper and better than they do, if they only knew how to economize their food. You have told them how, but they are slow to learn, or loth to change from foolish old practices."

"What was your next change?"

"Oh, yes, I was about to tell you that. Well, I went to the butcher's the night before, and bought five cents' worth of little scrap pieces of lean beef, and I declare I think I got as much as a pound, and this I cut up into bits, and soaked over night—an all-important process for soup or a stew—cooking it in the same water. Then I bought two cents' worth of potatoes and one cent's worth of meal—that made the eight cents; two had to go for fuel every day, and the paper I got my purchases in served for kindling. The meal I wet up into stiff dough, and worked out into little round balls, about as big as grapes, and the potatoes I cut up into slices, and all together made a stew, or chowder, seasoned with a small onion and part of a pepper-pod that I got with the potatoes. It was very good, but it did not go quite so far as the soup either day, or else the fresh meat tasted so good that we wanted to eat more. But I can tell you, small as it may seem to you, there is a great deal of good eating in one Dime."

So there is—what a pity everybody don't know it! What a world of good might be done with a Dime!

Reader, have you got a Dime—that is, to spare—only one Dime? Give it to that poor widow. Give it! No; you owe it. She has given you twice its value, whether you are one that will feast to-day on a dollar, or be stinted with a Dime. She has taught you —what you never knew before—the value of one Dime.

What a pity so many should be thrown away! What a pity we could not teach this lesson of economy in food to the thousands who will suffer before spring for the Dimes wasted, through ignorance, when Dimes were plenty! Knowing how to use a Dime might often save a family from suffering—from beggary—from degradation. 'Tis a small coin. What if you invest it here, and give this article to those who would profit by learning how they can live, and satisfy the hunger of five persons, all day—for one Dime.

Yes, it is a small coin—ten will buy this book. What if you invest it, and give the book to some one who will profit by its lessons. Some have already. So hope we all will, and that it will be to them dimes saved ; so that all who give will feel that it is only paying a debt; as a correspondent does, who says: "I feel that I owe that poor widow ten dimes for what she has taught me about economy in living. As far as the matter of providing daily food for herself and family is concerned, she is probably independent; but she wants to properly clothe and educate those four dear little ones. Please hand her the inclosed. I have never yet been driven to the alternative of limiting myself and family to one solitary Dime a day ; but do not know how soon such may be the case, when our legislators are doing so much to strangle the energies of our industrial population."

Now this is one of the pleasant evidences

that this article upon economy in food is doing its mission.

But I must tell the writer that I did not do with his dollar as he bid me. I did not give it to *that* poor woman. Before I could see her, another came—one I knew—one who did live neat and respectable, and respected by all who knew her, as wife or widow of an honest, hard-working city carpenter; who dying, as we all must, left her, at thirty-eight years old, with five children under fifteen.

What a task—a living death! Dying that they might live. With feeble health—a toil-worn and torn constitution—her children sickly—sick for want of accustomed food and comforts that came with the father's daily wages, and were daily spent, so that when death came, and custom—fashion, with its inexorable law—demanded a costly coffin and an expensive "last home" in consecrated ground for the dead, there was no living left for the living—no home and food and fire for a family of whom it had been said, "How well they live!" Yes, they lived well, as the word goes—they did not live by the laws of economy. It was a lesson never taught in their school. It was a need they had never needed. They need it now. Now, when a Dime is more than a dollar then.. Now, when for one whole week, for that feeble, tender-reared American woman—and for four hungry children, who never, till their father's death, knew the want of a full meal; they have known it often since—for a whole week, the only food that entered the widow's desolate home, was two dimes' worth of dear bakers' bread.

The only fire was made of two pecks of coal. For food and fuel for five persons, not five, but seven days, three dimes and a half was all they had, and that was not economically expended, as was the Dime of which you read, because the woman did not understand the art; and it was no time to learn it, and her children starving the while. Just as well might you tell the drowning man to hold on, and you would read him a dissertation upon the art of swimming. Just as well might you tell the hungry dog that the bone he stole to him was useless, because he knew not the art of making soup. Three dimes and a half a week for a whole family! That is not the art of economy—it is the art of starving to death without dying. It might sustain a family in the woods of Kentucky, where fuel is worthless, and corn but a Dime a bushel, as I have often seen it sold. It is dearer now—very much dearer here—and no teaching of economy can tell a woman how to live upon so little.

It was to this woman that I gave the man's ten dimes. I gave her, too, what another "friend of the poor" had sent me—some clothes and shoes for her children; for of the latter they had none, and of the former, only the garb that makes them feel they are but beggars. Yet they are not—they are true-born American children. Perhaps, children of parents that did not practice economy, and did not lay up a store out of dimes wasted. Yet these should not be left to waste. It is poor economy to waste good flesh and blood—hands, heads, hearts, souls of our fellow-creatures.

Yet, without the economy of saving such

from waste, to worse than waste they must go.

Economy in food would save all from want.

Economy in clothes would clothe all the destitute.

Economy in drink would make all rich, for that is all waste.

There are six thousand drinking places in New York city. At many of these, every drink is a Dime. One hundred dimes a day for the average sales is within the limits of truth. SIXTY THOUSAND DOLLARS!

The amount drank at private tables is as much more. The loss of time and property, counting all the lives that rum has slain, is sixty thousand more, among our six hundred thousand people, every day.

Work out the sum; see how much it is per week—per month—per year—and then tell me if economy in drink would not make all rich, or, at least, leave none in want of bread. it would make a fund to feed the poor.

A Dime for a cigar! What of it?

Simply that it is not economy. Whether

a dime or a mill, it is, in a year, ten millions of dimes wasted.

Go count the stores on Broadway that sell cigars only, and see how many that pay a thousand dollars—ten thousand dimes a year for rent alone!

Then count in one walk from the Battery to Union Square, how many men—men!—boys—bipeds—things with hair and legs, that are burning out life and cigars at the same time, and you will readily believe that there is in this city one hundred thousand men—if men they be—who burn up a Dime a day in tobacco.

How much is that a year? Three hundred and sixty-five thousand dimes—thirty-six thousand five hundred dollars! How many poor women and children that would feed and clothe, and send to school, to church, and into the ways of life, and hope, and happiness, to be men and women, and not pining slaves of want, living upon a Dime a day!

How many lessons of economy would all these wasted dimes teach! They teach us one great lesson now. It is this: it is not economy to smoke. And perchance some of those who will puff the fetid odor of their bad breath and tobacco in your face while you read of this great waste of dimes, will laugh at your study and practice of economy in living, and die and leave their families to live, as best they may, upon a Dime a day.

ECONOMY IN FUEL.—So here let us give them another lesson in economy—*the economy in making a fire*—not at the end of a cigar, for in that there is no economy, however made; yet in that economy might be practiced—but in making a fire in the family stove, range, or grate, where anthracite coal is used.

Coal will not ignite without being first heated to a red heat with wood. Wood is costly. A load—a city load—of pine wood costs about two and three-fourth dollars. It is called a third of a cord. It is hardly an honest fourth. It is two cents a pound. It is usually cut by the sawyer three times. It should be cut six. It never should be cut by hand. That is not economy. It is cut six times by machine for the same price of three by hand, and it is split finer and better, without additional cost, by an ax driven, like the saw, by steam.

It is no longer economy to buy wood by the load, and have it cut and split upon the pavement before your door, for two reasons: it costs more, and burns more. It never will be split fine enough. The finer the better, if part of it be mere splinters. Then a small piece of paper and a match will serve to kindle. Put the wood all in a close bunch in the middle of the grate, with a small quantity of small pieces of coal over it. When these are heated, add more, a little at a time, until all is hot, and you will have a good fire. Economy in kindling a fire will save one half the cost of wood. Enough may be saved in every family in kindling wood alone to give a peck of coal to some needy one every day.

'Tis a small bunch of wood that costs a Dime. I have sometimes seen it used to kindle one fire; and often seen the grate filled heaping full of coal that had to be all removed after the paper and wood had burned out, because the builder had never studied the art and economy of kindling a fire.

Never, whether rich or poor, suffer your cinders or unburned bits of coal to be wasted in the ash-barrel. Measure for measure, they are worth more than coal. Save them, soak them, try them. Water renovates the coke, and wet cinders upon a hot coal fire will make it hotter, and keep it so longer than fresh coal.

Saving cinders is not meanness, it is economy.

To learn how to kindle a fire, is learning a useful lesson for life. It is a useful study of economy. Remember its teachings, for the time may come when it will be worth to you more than a Dime.

Let me repeat, while you listen: in short, have your kindling wood short, and all in a close pile over your crumpled paper. If it is set up like a stack, all the better to ignite. Put on small coal in small quantities till your fire burns bright; then add wet cinders, and then you will save a Dime a day.

No young gent or lady should ever be allowed a servant to kindle a fire in their own room. It is bad economy. General Washington always kindled his own fire. Are you better than him? Besides the economy and advantage of learning the art of making a fire in your room, there is in the practice a positive economy of health.

Wasted Fuel.—The want of economy in fuel does not all belong to the city. We have a lesson for the country as well. It is the economy of chips.

Chips.—This is a small word, but it has a big meaning. What should we do without chips—chips of wood—not "chips and porridge," for that is poor diet—not "chips of the old block," for the old block is often an old blockhead—not, however, a greater one than he that has chips and does not save them carefully in a dry place to kindle his fire. Chips are equally valuable in town or country, yet they are the most wasted in the latter, for there they are left in the woods or at the wood-pile to rot, and by many farmers they are not even used for manure. Here in the city, those who make chips rarely save them, but there are hosts of men and women and little boys and girls constantly engaged in picking up every chip that is thrown in the street, or that the workman hews from his timber wherever they are permitted to come. So important are chips in the city, where nearly all our fuel is anthracite coal, that ingenious mechanics have built machines to make chips—to saw and split whole shiploads of wood into chips, which are sold by the barrel to families or retailed by the grocer in bundles. We have often noticed the eagerness with which the little folks, who are always looking out for a waif, seize upon a small strip that has been swept into the street. "Waste not a chip," should be a standing motto in every family in town and country. Country reader, have you a wood-house? And if you have, have you a storeroom for chips? If you have neither, you may be an honest man, and may not be a sloven, and may not have a scolding wife; but we want an indorser for your word upon all these points. No country house was ever complete in its arrangements that had not a chip-room where all the chips may be saved, and where dry kindling-wood can always be found. None of the many wastes about a farm are worse than the waste of chips. None of the conveniences of life are more convenient than chips. What a glorious fire is that in the great kitchen fireplace, made of a green log, a seasoned fir-stick and middle-wood, topped off with the two-bushel basket full of chips! But their great value is to kindle the fire, either in the old fireplace, or modern grate, or fashionable stove. Now is the season of making chips; now is the time to save chips —not by throwing them down at the bottom of the wood-house to mold and always be damp, but carefully laid up in a dry loft. Even with those who saw their wood, there are splinters and dry bits to save, and we have no doubt, when the economy of fuel is well understood, that all saw-dust will be saved and compounded with pitch, so as to make good kindling. But there is so much comfort in chips that we do not understand how anybody can waste them. Only think of the convenience of a handful of dry chips from the chip-room, next summer, to boil the teakettle. If you have no wood-house nor chip-room—and we believe a few farmers have neither—we conjure you to cut your summer fire-wood in winter—cut it up ready to burn, and pile it up in the form of a hay-stack, with the chips on top. So, you save your chips.

Now a word about the economizing of fuel in city and country. Open fireplaces and grates are the most wasteful of heat, though they are, probably, the most saving of health. Red-hot stoves in close rooms are among the abominations of the age. They save heat and waste health. The best plan to warm a house for a family is to place a large stove in the hall, and then you can have the room-doors open, and in moderate weather thus warm the rooms; and in colder days a small fire in a stove or grate in the room will make it comfortable, and give you a free circulation of air at the same time. Houses with "modern improvements," of course, are heated with hot-air furnaces; some of them are hot-air abominations. The perfection of heating our dwellings has not yet been reached, nor will it be, until we build them with hollow walls and floors, and double windows, and introduce heated air into all the cavities. As houses are now constructed and warmed, we not only waste the chips, but we waste one half the heat generated by our fuel. It is high time that, in more senses than one, we should save the chips.

We should like to know the per centage or waste of coal upon all that is burned in private houses in this city, where grates seem to have been constructed with, apparently, little or no object in view, except waste, both of heat sent up the chimney, and unburned coal sent to the ash-barrel.

The latter is so great as to afford constant employment to some thousand persons, who are constantly going about gathering the fragments of coal from the ashes; and still thousands of tons every year are carried off in the ash-carts to fill up and build out some wharf whereon to land more coal. The waste of heat in our consumption of fuel is, to say the least, full one half. In fact, if all the wasted heat of all our coal-burning fires in the city were saved and properly distributed, it is likely that the consumption would be reduced to one fourth the present quantity; because it has been demonstrated in the heating of large buildings, that heat could be carried any required distance in pipes, as well as gas or water, and by surrounding the pipes in the ground with suitable non-conducting substances, very little heat would be lost.

FIRE KINDLERS.—Melt three pounds of resin in a quart of tar, and stir in as much saw-dust and pulverized charcoal as you can, and then spread the mass upon a board till cool, and then break it into lumps as big as your thumb. You can light it with a match, and it will light a fire, for it burns with a strong blaze. It is economical of time and money. It may cost three shillings, and save ten shillings' worth of wood.

CHAPTER XI.

ECONOMY IN FOOD—WHAT SHALL WE EAT?

[*Published in The Tribune, Nov.* 14, 1855.]

Economy in Food—Remedy for Hunger—Abuses of our Market System—Economy in Buying—Fashionable Beef —Nutrition in Food—What shall we Buy?—Cheap Food —Incontrovertible Facts—How to Cook Hominy—Hominy Recipes—A Corn Meal Loaf—What shall we Eat? etc.

WITH the present prices of rent, fuel, meat bread, flour, meal, sugar, potatoes, and other staple articles of supply for a family in New York, it only requires but a slight insight into the condition of all the laboring class to see that the cry frequently raised for an increase of wages is only the disguised cry of the hungry for food. Daily wages are daily consumed; and often the only means of support for a week is the weekly credit of the butcher, baker, and grocer. This is never given except at an increased profit, and a little too often at a profit obtained by palpable swindling in light weights and measures, of which the victims dare not complain, for fear of losing the "accommodation," as the credit is called. While work lasts the laborer can live; when it fails, he has nothing in store to fall back upon. Whoever, then, will make known to this class how to economize in their food, so as to increase the supply without an increase of expenditure, will be doing them a greater benefit than he would in a life-long harangue on politics, either Hard Shell, Soft Shell, or no shell.

We need not repeat here how hard it is for those dependent upon daily employment to furnish their families with suitable food, at a time when, from sickness or other cause, they are not in receipt of wages.

Too often, at such times, there is deep suffering; and sometimes actual starvation.

Will it be any better next winter, now so rapidly approaching, that it sends a shudder through many a family circle who remember what scenes they have passed through in January, February, and March?

There has been, there is now, there will be much suffering for food in this city, notwithstanding our receipts of tens of thousands, weekly, of butchers' animals, and our millions of bushels of corn, and wheat, and rye, and oats, and barley, and buckwheat, and beans, and peas, and rice, for breadstuffs, and daily ship-loads of potatoes of both kinds, and untold piles of other edible roots and vegetables, and great storehouses full of flour, butter, cheese, fish, fruit, eggs, poultry, and salted meats, and a thousand unnamed articles of food ; yet the mass are not full fed, and why? Because they do not know how to eat. Not that they lack the animal function of consuming ; but in providing, both in the purchase of kind and quality, and in the preparation, there is a lamentable want of judgment, and utter want of economy. The want of food among the poor is a great evil. It breeds discontent, dissipation, crime, and ruin to any civilized society.

There is a remedy.

It would be greater charity to teach that remedy than to establish soup-houses.

The first step would be to change our fashion of food ; to abandon such articles as are excessively dear in the raw state, for others equally good and more nutritious, and to adopt a different and more rational plan of cooking. This would not only promote economy, but health; both of which would add vastly to our stock of enjoyment.

Without exception, both rich and poor in America eat extravagantly of animal food, cooked in the most extravagant and wasteful manner; by frying, baking, roasting, or boiling, and throwing away half of the nutritious matter in burned gravy, or gelatine dissolved in the pot liquor.

Again, we consume vast quantities of the meanest and most innutritious vegetables, costly at first, and cooked in the most foolishly wasteful manner. The fashion of extravagance in living is set by the rich, and they are aped in their folly by the poor. The consequence is, that there are want and suffering whenever work and wages fail.

There is a remedy. The only question is, how it shall be applied? Better than charity would be organizations, not to provide food for the poor, but to teach them what to buy, and how to use it; how to economize their money.

The very first step toward this blessed state of things should be taken by our city government, if indeed we have such a thing left to us, by removing all restrictions upon the producer, by which he is kept away from the consumer. We pay now an average of thirty-three per cent. advance upon every thing that is eaten in New York, over and above what we should pay if these restrictions were removed.

Let every one who has bought a head of cabbage this fall, think what he paid. Six, ten, or twelve cents each, while the producer has not received an average of two cents each. The turnip-eaters are paying every day at the rate of one to two dollars a bushel. The producer is receiving an average of less than twenty cents. We pay for many things in the same proportion, owing to our absurd and wicked market regulations.

The producer is kept away from the consumer. He is not permitted to come into the city and enjoy the advantages of "free trade" in his own produce. Why? The city fathers say we have no room—nowhere for him to stand his wagon, where the poor man or the poor woman may come with her market basket upon her arm, and get it filled at first prices.

Under the present market regulations, all the country wagons are huddled into the cramped space around Washington Market, where none but stout men, or a class of market bullies can get to them; for, in addition to the crowding, the wagons are driven out at seven o'clock in the morning. The city fathers say they can not amend this error, because they have nowhere else to put the wagons. Give producers a chance to sell to consumers, and it will cheapen family marketing in this city to a very large class of consumers, full twenty-five per cent. Make a market-place for country wagons, and there let them stand and sell their stuff from sunrise till ten o'clock, at retail, with no privilege, until after that hour, of selling at wholesale, or leaving the stand, unless their load is all sold out.

This is a measure of relief to the poor, easily brought about; one that would produce real economy in food.

Our city makes paupers, first by thwarting the laborer in his facilities to get cheap food, and then by the soup-house system of feeding those who are unable, through misfortune, to obtain a supply.

But this is foreign to our main subject—economy in kind and quality of food for the industrious poor.

They do not study economy in their purchases. All kinds of fresh meat cost from ten to twenty cents a pound, and very few Americans are willing to take low price meats; and generally those who can least afford it, call for a rib roast, or a loin steak of beef, or a leg of lamb or mutton, or a loin of veal or pork; and rarely for the most economical pieces. A rib roast of six pounds for a dollar, in a poor man's family, is slightly extravagant; the cooking more so. The Jews' religion in eating meat is founded on true economy. They eat only the fore quarters, and sell the more expensive, and less valuable hind quarters, to the Gentiles. The fore quarter will not cut steaks and roasts equal to the hind quarter, but it is more economical for soups, stews, pot-pies, or cooking in any form with vegetables and gravy. The following exhibit will show those who will have nothing but choice cuts of beef why they have to pay so high for them—it is because nobody will buy any thing but choice cuts. It is the universal complaint of all the first-class butchers that they can not sell their coarse meat, and "plates and navels" are a drug upon the packer's hands at six cents a pound. Now a good bullock, whose quarters will weigh 800 pounds, will cut up and sell at about the following figures:

	Weight.	Price per lb.	Amount.
Ribs	130	13c.	$16 90
Hips and loins	130	13	16 90
Chucks	140	6	8 40
Buttocks, rump, and socket	130	9	11 70
Plates and navel	90	6	5 40
Shoulders, clods, and brisket	100	6	6 00
Tops of sirloin and fat	40	9	3 60
Legs and shins	46	3	1 05
Total	800	..	$69 95

	Weight.	Price per lb.	Amount.
Hide	85	5	$4 25
Fat	90	8	7 20
Tongue, 50c.; feet, 25c.			75
The bullock, at 10c. per lb., costs $80—sells for...			$83 15

Now it is a fact that a great portion of the above, rated at six, eight, and nine cents, is equally good, and would be more economical, at the same price per pound, than that rated at thirteen cents; but fashion dictates, and folly buys ribs and loins, and for this the butcher must charge high, because he can not get any body to buy the other parts at cost. And so fashion and folly keep up the price of beef. The man or woman with scanty means, to fill the market basket, not only buys dear meats, but crude, innutritious vegetables, such as cabbage, turnips, and potatoes; for, notwithstanding so many persons think potatoes a necessary article of food, they are not an economical one; and all the cruder substances of vegetable food, though necessary and healthful, should not be sought after because cheap, to save money.

The most economical mode of preparing

food is a due mixture of meat and vegetable substance in the form of soups; but no man should live upon soup alone, any more than he should upon meat or fine flour bread. Health, as well as appetite, requires variety. It happens, now that breadstuffs, notwithstanding the high price of bread and flour, are the cheapest of all human food; and it also happens that by our slavery of fashion we do not use the cheapest kinds of this kind of cheap food.

The following are the retail prices of some of the principal articles of food in New York, Oct., 1855:

Flour, per bbl..........	$12 00	per lb., 6¼c.
Sago..................	—	" " 8 to 9c.
Farina...............	—	" " 12 to 15c.
Bread.................	—	" " 6¼c.
Corn meal, per cwt......	2 75 to $3 00	" " 3½c.
Buckwheat meal, per cwt.	3 00 to $3 50	" " 3½ to 4c.
Barley meal, per cwt.....	3 00	" " 3½ to 4c.
Oatmeal, per cwt........	4 00 to $4 50	" " 5 to 6¼c.
Rye flour, per bbl.	7 00	" " 4 to 4½c.
Hominy, per cwt........	4 00	" " 5c.
Cracked wheat, per cwt. .	5 50	" " 6c.
Split peas, per bushel....	2 25	" " 4½c.
Whole peas, per bushel...	2 50	" " 5c.
White beans, per bushel..	2 00	" " 4½ to 5c.
Dried sweet corn, per bus.	4 50	" " 10 to 12½.
Rice, per cwt.	5 00	" " 6 to 7c.

Potatoes, per bbl., $1 50 to $1 75; per bushel, 75 cents; per lb., 1½c.

Macaroni and vermicelli, 11 to 12 cents per lb.

Sugar, 8 to 11 cents per lb.

Butter, per lb , averages 28 cents. Cheese, 12 to 14 cents.

Apples, per bbl., $2 to $3 50; per bushel, $1 average.

All kinds of meat, salt and fresh, and all sorts of fish, will average 12½ cents a pound to the buyer of small quantities.

Eggs are worth 25 cents per dozen, which is about 18 cents per lb. A dozen eggs, average size, will weigh one pound six ounces.

Turnips, per bushel, 25 cents; carrots, 50 cents; beets, 50 cents; onions, 75 cents; cabbage, about 2 cents a pound.

Dried fruits, per lb.—Apples, 7 to 8 cents; pears, 15 to 20 cents; plums, 8 to 14 cents; cherries, 15 to 20 cents; peaches, 15 to 18 cents; raisins, 8 to 12½ cents.

The following is the proportion of nutritious matter and water in each of the following substances:

Lbs.	Substances.	Lbs. nut. mat.	Lbs. water.
100	Wheat flour	90	10
100	Corn meal	91	9
100	Rice	86	14
100	Barley meal	88	12
100	Rye flour	79	21
100	Oatmeal	75	25
100	Potatoes	22½	77½
100	White beans	95	5
100	Carrots	10	90
100	Turnips	4½	95½
100	Cabbage	7½	92½
100	Beets	15	85
100	Strawberries	10	90

Lbs.	Substances.	Lbs. nut. mat.	Lbs. water.
100	Pears	16	84
100	Apples	16	84
100	Cherries	25	75
100	Plums	29	71
100	Apricots	26	74
100	Peaches	20	80
100	Grapes	27	73
100	Melons	3	97
100	Cucumbers	2½	97½

Meats, generally, are about three fourths water, and milk, as it comes from the cow, over ninety per cent. How is it as it comes from the milkmen?

It is true that this chemical analysis does not give us the exact comparative value of food, but with that, and the prices of the various articles, it can not be a hard matter to determine what is the cheapest or most economical kind of food for us to use.

Perhaps of all the articles named, taking into account the price and nutritious qualities, oatmeal will give the greatest amount of nutriment for the least money. But where will you find it in use? Not one family in a thousand ever saw the article; not one in a hundred ever heard of it, and many who have heard of it have a vague impression that none but starving Scotch or Irish ever used it; and, in short, that oats, in America, are only fit food for pigs and horses.

It is a great mistake. Oatmeal is excellent in porridge, and all sorts of cooking of that sort, and oatmeal cakes are sweet, nutritious, and an antidote for dyspepsia. Just now, we believe oats are the cheapest of any grain in market, and it is a settled fact that oats give the greatest amount of power of any grain consumed by man or beast.

This cheap food only needs to be fashionable, to be extremely popular among all laborers, all of whom, to say nothing of other classes, eat too much fine flour bread.

Cracked wheat and loaf bread cost the same price, or perhaps a less price for the wheat by the pound. A pound of the wheat, properly cooked, is worth more than four pounds of bread.

Hominy, samp, hulled corn, we have so often recommended and urged upon the attention of all, both rich and poor, as cheap, wholesome, nutritious food, that we have induced many to try it, who would not give it up now under any consideration. We reiterate all that we have ever said in its favor. Thirty years' experience in its use only serves to confirm us in the opinion that it is such excellent and economical food, that too much can not be said in its favor. The only thing necessary in its cooking, is to cook it enough —it can not be cooked too much.

Every family should eat beans and peas, because of all articles they afford the most nutriment for the least money.

One pound of cheap meat, say at ten cents, and one pound of split peas, say five cents, will give a fuller dinner to a family than a dollar expended for beefsteak and white bread. This is a kind of economy that should be known, and rigidly practiced.

One bushel of white beans will feed more laboring men than eight bushels of potatoes. The beans will cost two dollars, potatoes six.

A single quart of beans costs nine cents; a half pound of salt pork, six cents; a pound of hominy, five cents; and that will give a meal to a larger family than a dollar's worth of roast beef, white bread, potatoes, and other vegetables.

We would not confine the laborer or the poorest family to this cheap food; but we do insist that it is their duty to substitute such food, occasionally, in place of that which is more expensive, and thus, by saving, lay up a few dollars in the savings bank to save themselves from the mere life-saving contrivance, the soup-house.

We hope never to see another of these pauper-making establishments in operation again in this city. Let men think twice before they open another one.

But let every one think of the economy of making a soup-house at home. We spoke of pea-soup. Is there any living witness of that good old Yankee dish of cheap food, called bean porridge? Let it be revived in every family—among the rich as a luxury, and among the poor as an article of economy.

There is another Yankee dish besides bean soup and baked beans that we should like to see revived, and that is the baked Indian-meal pudding; and this brings us to Indian bread, a mixture of two thirds corn meal and one third rye meal, not rye flour, which makes most delicious bread at less than one half the cost of wheat flour.

We could go on a long time pointing out the errors of living, in which economy is lost sight of, if we thought the wished-for effect would be produced. We urge all to think of what we have said, and that one of the best things that can be done for the poor is to teach them practical economy in every-day life.

No charitable societies have ever done so much good to the poor by the distribution of food as they could do by printing and putting into the hands of every family a little tract containing practical lessons of economy in the art of living well and living cheap—an art that would prevent the waste of food, and lessen the expense of first purchases, and increase the nutritious qualities, while it added immensely to the table enjoyment of every family.

In a great majority of cases it may be set down as an incontrovertible fact that want comes of waste, and waste comes of want of knowledge of the properties of different articles of food, and how to combine them so as to produce the most beneficial effect.

It may be set down as another incontrovertible fact, that no class of people can want food and remain virtuous. Their degeneracy, both physically and morally, is certain. It is our religious duty, then, to study and teach economy in food, and the art of living better and cheaper; more in accordance with the principles that promote health, vigor, intellectual capacity, comfort, happiness, and morality of the human family.

How much good would come of it if we should practice upon the text that forms the title of this article! Let those who read and think first set the example; the unthinking will follow, and their children will rise up and call them blessed.

I think that I can afford to devote one chapter to a dissertation upon

HOMINY.

Hominy we have before given our opinion

upon. It is an article that no family, desirous of practicing economy, can do without. It is a very cheap, healthy, nutritious food. It usually costs only half the price per pound of flour, and contains no moisture, while the best of flour holds from twelve to sixteen pounds of water in a barrel.

I have known potatoes, hominy, and white beans to be all sold at the same price, $2 50 a bushel, and rice but a little dearer. If a man can afford to eat fried gold for breakfast, boiled bank-notes for dinner, and roasted dollars for supper, he can afford to eat potatoes cooked in the same way, and not otherwise, at such high prices. In point of economy as human food, one bushel of beans or hominy is equal to ten of potatoes.

It is surprising how little is known of this nutritious, healthy food; and what an excellent substitute it is for potatoes during the continuance of the disease among them, which renders some that are fair to the eye unfit for food, and all exceedingly dear, even at the present rate of about one dollar and a half a bushel as an average cost to the consumer in New York, in December, 1855.

Hominy, too, is a dish almost as universally liked as potatoes, and at the South it is more freely eaten; while at the North it is seldom seen. In fact, it is an unknown food except to a few persons in cities. By hominy, we do not mean a sort of coarse meal, but grains of white corn from which the hull and chit, or eye, has been removed by moistening and pounding in a wooden mortar, or patent hulling machine, leaving the grains almost whole, and composed of little else but starch. It has often been said, not one cook in ten knows how to boil a potato. We may add another cipher when speaking of the very simple process of cooking hominy. We give the formula from our own experience, and from instructions received in a land where "hog and hominy" are well understood. Wash slightly in cold water, and soak twelve hours in tepid, soft water, then boil slowly from three to six hours in same water, with plenty more added from time to time with great care to prevent burning. *Don't salt while cooking*, as that or *hard water* will harden the corn; so it will peas or beans, green or dry, and rice also. When done, add butter and salt; or a better way is to let each one season to suit the taste. It may be eaten with meat in lieu of vegetables, or with milk, sugar, or syrup. It is good, hot or cold, and the more frequently it is warmed over, it is like the old-fashioned pot of

> "Bean porridge hot, or bean porridge cold,
> Bean porridge best at nine days old."

So is hominy; it is good always, and very wholesome, and, like tomatoes, only requires to be eaten once or twice to fix the taste in its favor.

In this city the article is called samp, and the name hominy is given to corn cracked in a mill, and winnowed and sifted, and numbered according to its fineness.

It is cheap, healthy food. I have thought proper to add a few of the ways in which hominy may be used.

HOMINY BREAKFAST CAKES.—Mash the cold hominy with a rolling-pin, and add a little flour-and-milk batter, so as to make the whole thick enough to form into little cakes in the hand, or it may be put upon the griddle with a spoon. Bake brown, eat hot, and declare you never ate any thing better of the batter-cake kind.

Hominy and Milk, hot or cold, is as much better than mush and milk as that is better than rye-meal porridge.

Hominy Pudding.—Prepare as for batter cakes, add one egg to each pint, some whole cinnamon, sugar to suit the taste, and a few raisins, and bake like rice pudding. A little butter or chopped suet may be added. Serve hot or cold, with or without sauce.

Hominy Salad.—To a pint of cold hominy add a small onion, a quarter of a boiled chicken, or about the same quantity of lobster, chopped fine, to which some add a small pickle. To be dressed with sweet oil, mustard, pepper, and vinegar. It is a very good substitute for green salads at seasons when the latter can not be obtained.

Hominy and Beans.—Mix equal parts of cold baked beans and hominy together, and heat up, and you will have an excellent dish.

Hominy Beating.—We presume we have heard of a still evening, while floating in our skiff down the Ohio River, in days

"Long, long ago,"

a hundred hominy mortars in operation, as this is or was a common occupation of the negroes' evenings, beating their favorite food.

Of late years, throughout the South, the ground hominy, or cracked corn, has in a great measure driven the old hominy mortar out of use. This is cooked in the same way, by soaking and boiling, until it becomes gelatinous, and then, when cold, if cut in slices and fried in a little fat, will often be eaten in preference to any other bread.

At the South, negroes prefer corn meal to wheat flour, pound for pound. It is ground very coarse, and frequently eaten, hulls and all, in preference to sifting.

The full allowance for a laboring man or woman—one that toils all the hours of daylight in the field—is a peck and a half of corn meal and three and a half pounds of fat bacon. In the cotton States the average price of the corn is about seventy-five cents a bushel, and the price of the bacon eight cents a pound. This would make the week's rations cost fifty-six cents a week. At still higher rates, it would not be a dime a day; in many places, not half that. In many places, though, the negroes do not get half the above rations. In this city a peck and a half of meal and three and a half pounds of bacon would average a cost of ninety cents. Few would be willing to live upon that alone. It would not be good economy to do so. It would be good economy for us all to use more Indian corn meal. I offer to those who will try the economy as well as palatableness of a loaf of wheat and Indian bread, the following good receipt:

To two quarts of Indian meal add boiling water enough to wet the same; when sufficiently cooled, add one teaspoonful of salt, half a pint of yeast, one teaspoonful of saleratus, one half teacupful of molasses, and flour enough to form it into a loaf (it should not be kneaded hard); when light, bake two hours in a well-heated oven. (It should be baked until brown.)

All corn bread should be cooked a long time. The negroes often bury the dough in the hot embers all night.

Economy in cooking is as much required as economy in purchasing the food.

Domestic happiness is greatly dependent upon the manner in which the cooking department of the household is managed, whether by the mistress or a hireling.

A cook who can make a good loaf of bread, boil a potato aright, or broil a mutton chop properly, is one of a thousand, and perhaps she would not know how to make a pot of mush, because it is so seldom made, where its use would promote both health and economy.

Despising household duties is one of the sins of American women. A woman need not be a drudge, or slave to care, but still be the director of all the household affairs. The woman, whatever her position and wealth, who attends to her own housekeeping affairs, reaps her reward in improved health and freedom from lassitude, which she suffers through neglect of exercise.

Many a mother has unwittingly pampered her children's appetites till she has created disease, and inbred into their natures profligacy and selfishness. If the economy of food was understood, it would save many errors. Nothing that is unwholesome for children should be ever set before them.

How many doctors' bills are made by inattention to diet!

This is poor economy. So it is to despise any of the little matters about household expenses, that would save the expenditure of money.

Look how much you could save in a year, or decade of years, by this simple text—

WHAT SHALL WE EAT?

It is one of the most frequent and most unanswerable questions in the human family.

With a hard winter—every winter is hard for the poor—before us—with the cold winds of the dreary month of December peering into every crack of our houses—with labor scarce and wages low, particularly to every woman who depends upon the work of her fingers for food—with a large population out of employment—with suffering staring all in the face who depend upon daily wages, and make no daily provision for a day of trouble—with the price of food, and fuel, and rent as high as it is in this city, it behooves every one to inquire: *What shall we eat?*

When wages are two dollars a day, the laboring man may eat roast beef and plum pudding; but if he does so often, he knows little of economy.

We can not cheapen food, but we can eat cheaper food; and whatever will tend to teach those who look long at a Dime before they spend it, what to buy, will be to them a blessing. Whatever I can show them what to eat, less expensive than their accustomed diet, should be at once adopted. Although I may repeat something said before in these pages, I shall make the following suggestions upon this page:

Fresh meat of all kinds, at the prices at which butchers retail it, is not economical food. Meats will average over a shilling a pound. Salted meats are cheaper than fresh. In economizing food, meat should never be fried or boiled. If you would get the most substance out of fresh meat, make it into soup, or stew, or pot-pie. In making soup, soak your meat some hours in cold water, and boil it in the same. Thicken with beans, peas, rice, barley, hominy, or broken bread. The best meat is the most economical for soup. Do not buy bones.

If you boil meat to eat, never put it in cold water. Let it be boiling when you put the meat in the pot. Do not buy fresh meat a pound or two at a time. Buy a quarter or half a sheep. You get it at half price. Beef or pork by the quarter is a quarter cheaper.

True, the woman with the Dime can not partake of this advantage. Many families can that do not. Many could unite, one with another, and buy at wholesale rates. It is a kind of economy, worth more than a Dime. Look at the "flour leagues" that have been formed in the Eastern States, by which families have obtained their flour one or two dollars cheaper in a barrel. So the man who studies economy may save a dime here, a dollar there, which at last will amount to an eagle.

A dollar saved upon a barrel of flour is equal to a gift of sixteen loaves of bakers' bread. But, I repeat, do not buy your bread ready baked. It is sixpence a pound. Dry flour is the same price. Home-made bread is far more nutritious.

RYE AND INDIAN BREAD.—Here is a good receipt for making this cheap, wholesome bread:

Stir and mix most thoroughly two quarts of Indian corn meal with a tablespoonful of salt and a quart of boiling water, or enough to wet every grain of meal. When the mush cools to milk-warm, stir in one quart of rye meal, and a teacupful of good yeast, which you will first mix with half a pint of warm water, so that the yeast will be more evenly diffused. With the rye meal add water enough to make the mass a stiff dough, but not as hard or tough as flour. It must be kneaded with the hands. [*Remember—rye meal is not rye flour.* It is the product of the whole grain.] Put the dough in a pan, and pat it smooth with a wet hand. It will rise in an hour, in a warm place, enough to bake, and should be put in a hot oven, and remain three hours; or, if all night, all the better.

We should make greater use of home-made bread, and then we should escape the deleterious adulterations of the baker, not half of which have I mentioned.

Every family, whether rich or poor, or in town or country, should make it a religious duty to make use of more corn meal, oatmeal, Graham flour, hominy, and cracked wheat for bread, in preference to fine wheat flour, both for health and economy. Look at the relative retail prices per pound of these articles on page 310, and see which will give the most nutriment for the least money; not which will afford you the most fashionable bread. If white fine flour was not fashionable, or if people did not think that brown bread has a look of poverty, we should have the brown bread upon every table, for it is not only more economical, it is more nutritious and more healthy, particularly for children.

We do not eat oatmeal in this country to any extent, and yet it is the most nutritious breadstuff ever used by man. Look at the Scotch with their oatmeal porridge—as robust a set of men as ever lived.

A Highlander will scale mountains all day upon a diet of oatmeal stirred with his finger in water, fresh from a gurgling spring, in a leather cup. Another excellent, though little used breadstuff, particularly for the sedentary, or persons of costive habits, is cracked wheat, or wheaten grits, as the article is called. That and Graham flour should be used in preference, at the same price per pound, to white flour, because more healthy and more nutritious. One hundred pounds of Graham flour is worth full as much in a family as one hundred and thirty-three pounds of superfine white flour. Corn meal usually costs less than half the price of flour. It is worth twice as much. It is not so economical in summer, because it takes so much fire to cook it. The first great error in preparing corn meal is in grinding it too much, and next in not cooking it enough. Corn meal mush should boil two hours; it is better if boiled four, and not fit to eat if boiled less than one hour. Buckwheat flour should never be purchased by a family who are obliged to economize food. It is dear at any price, because it must be floated in dear butter to be eaten, and then it is not healthy. Oatmeal makes as good cakes as buckwheat, and far more nutritious. But it is more nutritious, and is particularly healthy for children, in the form of porridge.

Pork and Beans.—Perhaps I run the risk of ridicule by reiterating here, what I have so often asserted, that white beans, at the ordinary prices, in most places, if not all, are the cheapest, because the most nutritious of all vegetables. Beans enter very largely into the diet of the inhabitants of some countries. This is particularly the case in Mexico. Baked beans, with salt pork, used to be one of the most common dishes in New England. I have read somewhere that Professor Liebig has stated that pork and beans form a compound of substances peculiarly adapted to furnish all that is necessary to support life, and give bone, muscle, and fat, in proper proportions, to a man. This food will enable one to perform more labor, at less cost, than any other substance. A quart of beans, eight cents, half a pound of pork, six cents, will feed a large family for a day, with good strengthening food.

BEAN PORRIDGE is another of the old-fashioned dishes of New England. We should call it bean soup now. Four quarts of beans and two pounds of corned beef, "boiled to rags" in fifty quarts of water, would give a good meal to fifty men—one cent a meal.

POTATOES NOT CHEAP FOOD.—Potatoes should be utterly abandoned by the poor, when a dollar a bushel is the selling price. They can not afford to eat them. Potatoes sell, at wholesale, for an average of two dollars a barrel, which is eighty-seven and a half cents a bushel. At retail, the poor pay two dollars a bushel, or about four cents a pound, which is about as much as corn meal; more than half as much as fine flour; nearly as much a bushel as beans, while one bushel of the latter are worth, for food, as much as a cart-load of potatoes. All other vegetables are still more uneconomical than potatoes. Carrots are the cheapest of all roots. But they are but little used as human food, though very nutritious. They are good, simple boiled, and eaten with a little butter or meat gravy. They should always form an ingredient of soup. They are sold by the quantity, at fifty cents a bushel. Turnips are dear at any price. There is more nutriment in a quart of carrots than in a bushel of turnips. They are eighty-two per cent. water. Cabbage is nutritious, but very expensive. Buy very little of it if your money is short. Dried sweet corn is an article that all persons are fond of. It sells for four dollars to five dollars a bushel, which weighs forty-two pounds, and would retail at about ten cents a pound. We don't know about the economy of eating it, as compared with other breadstuffs, but as compared with coarse vegetables it is immeasurably cheaper. A pound of sweet corn cooked to be eaten with meat, is worth more than three pounds of extra meat. It is also very excellent and nutritious mixed in the bean soup.

Another very excellent, nutritious, economical article of food is dried peas. They are generally a little more costly than beans, but some think they will go further. At any rate they are good for a change. It would be good for a change for those who are put to their wits' end to know how to get food enough to feed their families, if any thing that we have said shall put them in a way of changing some of their old habits, so as to buy such articles as will satisfy hunger, while giving them health and strength, for less than half the money they are now expending, though living only half comfortably.

That the laboring man *must* eat meat is a fallacy. I have seen thousands of laboring men, in South Carolina, who never eat meat. Thousands of others do not eat meat, or food made of meat, oftener than once a week. Half a bushel of sweet potatoes is a common allowance for rice-field hands a week. Sometimes it is a peck of rice, or meal, with soup, one day in the week, made by boiling fifteen pounds of meat, with crude vegetables, in eighty quarts of water. Upon such diet men are healthy, if not strong.

Dyspeptic persons may enjoy a full meal without meat vastly to their benefit. Bread and potatoes; or bread, potatoes, and apples; or bread, potatoes, apples, and squash; or a hundred other combinations. A full diet does not consist in any given number or kind of articles; but on the proper quantity and quality of some or all kinds of food. Because the appetite craves meat, does not prove it necessary, any more than the cravings of vitiated appetites after rum and tobacco. Still, I do not recommend all to discard meat. I only ask them to exercise more economy in its purchase and preparation.

Tea and Coffee.—As I do not discard meat from the poor man's diet, the poor woman will of course console herself with the hope that I shall not discard tea and coffee.

I will compromise the matter by allowing

her to retain *black tea*, if properly made, though it certainly is not a necessary article upon any table.

If black tea is steeped a few minutes in the usual way of making green tea, the decoction is acrid and unpalatable. If boiled steadily for fifteen to thirty minutes, the resinous substance is dissolved and the flavor entirely changed.

I never use green tea, and never recommend it to be used, because it is a manufactured article, frequently colored with deleterious drugs. COFFEE I never use, because experience taught me, by a long trial of daily use, and subsequent well-managed experiments upon myself, that it was the cause of all my severe suffering from nervous and sick headaches. Because I know this, I have discarded its use. Coffee is not food.

And certainly for all those who buy stuff called "ground coffee," I would recommend as equally nutritious, and far more healthy, a decoction of burned crusts, burned bran, burned rye, burned peas, burned carrots, and many other cheap substances; and if not aromatic enough, buy the "essence of coffee," and add a few drops. If not bitter enough, add quassia chips. If not astringent enough, you can get that quality from oak bark, cheaper than the coffee berry.

Asparagus seeds, treated just like coffee, make a decoction undistinguishable from the real Mocha or Java.

But as long as pure water pours down Niagara Falls, the same element may be poured down all our throats far more economically, and far more healthily, than any decoction of berries, roots, beans, grain, or any brewing or distillation of the same.

Of the economy of water used freely upon the exterior also, as well as for drink, I could not say too much, and yet have not room to say but these few words.

If you wash all over every morning with cold water as a regular habit, and use nothing but cold water for drink, you can work all day in a cold room without feeling the want of fire, and your health will be such that you will relish plain, coarse food, and thus will enjoy the benefit of economy in a three-fold sense.

VENTILATION.—Next to the neglect of water —and, in fact, it should rank first—is the neglect of air. The very worst economy is that which poisons people with dwellings that have no VENTILATION.

"Wherever we go, we find a lamentable ignorance of the laws which govern the human system. Among the laws of health, no one, perhaps, merits our serious attention more than that of fresh air. It may be said with truth, that not one building in a thousand, in this country, is properly ventilated. This is especially the case with regard to our school-houses, churches, halls, and other public buildings, where large bodies of people frequently congregate. In our churches it is almost impossible for any one not to be struck with the deficiency in means of ventilation; and even the slight means which are at hand are generally disregarded: the doors are closed, and windows kept down in stifling hot weather, as though fresh air were poison, and by no means to be inhaled except at long and painful intervals. A few moments' sitting convinces any one accustomed to breathing real and substantial air, that he is killing himself by degrees—a feeling of drowsiness overcomes him, and it requires an effort on his part to prevent himself from falling asleep, and nodding perhaps unwilling coincidence with the doctrines held forth in the pulpit. It is no extraordinary thing for us to see men and women asleep in church, and it is very common to hear people declaim against it as a sin of the first magnitude. In our opinion the sin consists in going where fresh air is a rarity, and thus inhaling poisonous and baleful air, to the great detriment of health and happiness. Let churches, school-houses, and all other public and private establishments, be ventilated properly, and there will be no difficulty in keeping people awake with a very ordinary sermon or lecture."

In all our tenant houses the same thing prevails in an aggravated form, and will continue until we have a Board of Health possessed of power to guard the health of the people.

WASTE.—What a little word this is; but what a big meaning it has! It seems to be in some way inseparably connected with every transaction and every act of our lives. Even life itself is one continual waste—animals and plants, from maturity to death; but that is natural waste—nature obeying nature's laws. The waste that we commit is unnatural and contrary to the laws of propriety and common sense.

Look into every kitchen; not only at the fat in the fire, but at the wasteful manner in which all of our cooking is done; besides the waste of food at the table. See how that delicate appetite—made delicate by waste—picks out a few choice morsels and carelessly casts the rest aside to go to waste.

It is safe to say that more food is wasted every day in this city than is eaten; not alone in the kitchen or at the table, but in our markets and store-houses, where whole cargoes of grain, meal, flour, meat, fish, fruits, and vegetables are continually being wasted through bad packing or bad management.

What a waste, too, are all of our retail purchases; and, because it is fashionable, buying food that wastes the most.

Is it any wonder that the poor suffer for food after committing such extravagant waste? Look at that man paying a dollar and a half—the price of a whole day's work —for a rib-roast of beef, to be cooked in the most wasteful way, when one half the money expended in a cheaper piece of meat, cooked in a different manner, with vegetables, bread, and gravy, would serve his family twice as long. But not so fashionable and genteel. No, and not so wasteful. Almost the whole system of American cookery is based upon a state of things that existed when we had such a surplus of food that the idea of waste was not taken into account.

There was a time, within but a few years past, at the West, when wheat could be purchased for twenty-five to forty cents a bushel, corn for ten or fifteen cents, pork for one to two cents a pound, and other things in proportion. It would be idle to talk to people about saving every iota of such cheap food.

To some extent the same cheapness has prevailed all over America, until the people have fallen into wasteful habits, both in keeping, cooking, and eating their food, that need reform.

It is probable that one half of the cooking in the kitchens of private families, in this city, is done by Irish servants, who possessed no higher art when they landed upon our shores than is required to boil and roast potatoes, or make an oatmeal cake or mess of porridge. The only art of saving they have any knowledge of is not to have any thing to save. All that should be saved is hurried out of sight in the basket of some of their own countrymen at the basement door, thereby encouraging another great waste—the waste of time of these lazy beggars.

Some men waste their lives in finding out cunning inventions, which they hide under a bushel, or in some other wasteful place, where their light never can shine out upon the world, for he wastes both time and money in not letting the world know where he keeps his wares for sale. Neglecting to advertise is a waste of common sense, and of that there is a greater waste than of all other commodities in this great community.

Finally, we have only touched upon food and fuel, the two most important items of waste in our economy of life, without touching a host of others equally deserving notice.

But we have said many things that may be read with profit by every person who loves neatness, order, economy, good food well cooked, and all the Home Comforts of life in city or country. And all such we ask to read this book, from title-page to

FINIS.

AMERICAN PHRENOLOGICAL JOURNAL.

A Repository of Science, Literature, and General Intelligence; Devoted to Phrenology, Physiology, Education, Mechanism, Agriculture, and to all those Progressive Measures which are calculated to Reform, Elevate, and Improve Mankind. Illustrated with Numerous Portraits and other Engravings. Quarto form, suitable for binding. Published Monthly, at One Dollar a Year.

It may be termed the standard authority in all matters pertaining to Phrenology, while the beautiful typography of the Journal, and the superior character of the numerous illustrations, are not exceeded in any work with which we are acquainted.—*Am. Cour.*

COMBE'S LECTURES ON PHRENOLOGY;

Including its appplication to the present and prospective condition of the United States. With Notes, an Essay on the Phrenological Mode of Investigation, and an Historical Sketch. By Andrew Boardman, M.D. Illustrated. Muslin, $1 25.

EDUCATION COMPLETE. Embracing

Physiology Animal and Mental, applied to the Preservation and Restoration of Health of Body and Power of Mind; Self Culture and Perfection of Character, including the Management of Youth; Memory and Intellectual Improvement, applied to Self Education and Juvenile Instruction. By Fowler. In 1 vol., $2 50.

Every one should read it who would preserve or restore his health, develop his mind and improve his character.

EDUCATION: Its Elementary Principles

founded on the Nature of Man. By J. G. Spurzheim, M. D. With an Appendix, containing a Description of the Temperaments, and an Analysis of the Phrenological Faculties. Price, in Paper, 62 cents. Muslin, 87 cents.

We regard this volume as one of the most important that has been offered to the public for many years. It is full of sound doctrines and practical wisdom.—*Boston Medical and Surgical Journal.*

MARRIAGE: Its History and Philoso-

PHY. With a Phrenological and Physiological Exposition of the Functions and Qualifications necessary for Happy Marriages. By L. N. Fowler. Illustrated. Paper, 50 cents; Muslin, 75 cents.

It contains a full account of the marriage forms and ceremonies of all nations and tribes, from the earliest history down to the present time. Those who have not yet entered into matrimonial relations, should read this book, and all may profit by a perusal. —*N. Y. Illustrated Magazine.*

SELF-CULTURE, AND PERFECTION OF

CHARACTER; including the Education and Management of Youth, By O. S. Fowler. Price, paper, 62 cents; Muslin, 87 cents.

"SELF-MADE, OR NEVER MADE," is the motto. No individual can read a page of it without being improved thereby. With this work, in connection with PHYSIOLOGY ANIMAL AND MENTAL, AND MEMORY AND INTELLECTUAL IMPROVEMENT, we may become fully acquainted with ourselves, comprehending, as they do, the whole man. We advise all to read these works.—*Com. School Advocate.*

RESULTS OF HYDROPATHY; OR, CONSTIPATION

not a Disease of the Bowels; Indigestion not a Disease of the Stomach; with an Exposition of the true Nature and Causes of these Ailments, explaining the reason why they are so certainly cured by the Hydropathic Treatment. By Edward Johnson, M. D. Muslin. Price, 87 cents.

WATER-CURE LIBRARY. In Seven Volumes,

12mo. Embracing the most popular works on the subject. By American and European Authors. Bound in Embossed Muslin. Price, only $7 00.

This library comprises most of the important works on the subject of Hydropathy. The volumes are of uniform size and binding, and form a most valuable medical library.

WATER AND VEGETABLE DIET in Consumption,

Scrofula, Cancer, Asthma, and other Chronic Diseases. In which the Advantages of Pure Water are particularly considered. By William Lambe, M. D., With Notes and Additions by Joel Shew, M. D. 12mo., 258 pp. Paper, 62 cents. Muslin, 87 cents.

ACCIDENTS AND EMERGENCIES: A

Guide, containing Directions for Treatment in Bleeding, Cuts, Bruises, Sprains, Broken Bones, Dislocations, Railway and Steamboat Accidents, Burns and Scalds, Bites of Mad Dogs, Cholera, Injured Eyes, Choking, Poison, Fits, Sun-stroke, Lightning, Drowning, etc., etc. By Alfred Smee, F. R. S. Illustrated with numerous Engravings Appendix by Dr. Trall. Price, prepaid, 15 cents.

PARENTS' GUIDE FOR THE TRANSMISSION

of the Desired Qualities to Offspring; and Childbirth made Easy By Mrs. Hester Pendleton. Price, 60 cents

PREGNANCY AND CHILDBIRTH. Illustrated

with Cases, Showing the Remarkable Effects of Water in Mitigating the Pains and Perils of the Parturient State. By Dr. Shew. Paper. Price, 30 cents.

INTRODUCTION TO THE WATER-CURE.

Founded in Nature, and adapted to the Wants of Man. Price, 15 cents.

SEXUAL DISEASES; their Causes, Prevention,

and Cure, on Physiological Principles. Embracing Home Treatment for Sexual Abuses; Chronic Diseases, especially the Nervous Diseases of Women; The Philosophy of Generation; Amativeness; Hints on the Reproductive Organs. In one volume. Price, $1 25.

THE SCIENCE OF HUMAN LIFE. By

Sylvester Graham, M.D. With a Portrait and Biography of the Author. $2 50.

CURIOSITIES OF COMMON WATER; or,

the Advantages thereof in preventing and curing Diseases; gathered from the Writings of several Eminent Physicians, and also from more than Forty Years' Experience. By John Smith, C. M. With Additions, by Dr. Shew. 30 cents.

PRACTICE OF WATER-CURE. With Au-thenticated Evidence of its Efficacy and Safety. Containing a detailed account of the various processes used in the Water-Treatment, etc. By James Wilson, M. D., and James M. Gully, M. D. 30 cents.

EXPERIENCE IN WATER-CURE. A Fa-miliar Exposition of the Principles and Results of Water-Treatment in Acute and Chronic Diseases; an Explanation of Water-Cure Processes; Advice on Diet and Regimen and Particular Directions to Women in the Treatment of Female Diseases, Water-Treatment in Childbirth, and the Diseases of Infancy. Illustrated by Numerous Cases. By Mrs Nichols. Price, 30 cents.

WATER-CURE MANUAL. A Popular Work, 12mo. Embracing descriptions of the various Modes of Bathing, the Hygienic and Curative Effects of Air, Exercise, Clothing, Occupation, Diet, Water-Drinking, etc. Together with Descriptions of Diseases, and the Hydropathic Remedies. By Joel Shew, M. D Muslin. Price, 87 cents.

CHRONIC DISEASES: Especially the Nervous Diseases of Women. By D. Rosch. Translated from the German. 30 cts.

ALCOHOLIC CONTROVERSY. A Review of the *Westminster Review* on the Physiological Errors of Teetotalism. By Dr. Trall. Price, 30 cents.

DIGESTION, PHYSIOLOGY OF, Consid-ered in Relation to the Principles of Dietetics By G. Combe. Illustrated, 30 cents.

FRUITS AND FARINACEA THE PROPER FOOD OF MAN. With Notes by Dr. Trall. Illustrated by numerous Engravings. $1 00.

VEGETABLE DIET: As Sanctioned by Medical Men, and by Experience in all Ages. Including a System of Vegetable Cookery. By Dr. Alcott. 87 cents.

SYRINGES.—We keep constantly for sale, at wholesale or retail, an assortment of the best Syringes, embracing a variety of styles, at different prices. The practical value of these instruments is becoming understood, and no family who have proper regard for health will be without one. We furnish with each instrument an ILLUSTRATED MANUAL of instructions, prepared by Dr. TRALL, giving complete directions for its use. The prices of the best syringes, sent by mail, postage pre-paid, are from $3 50 to $4 00.

FOWLER AND WELLS have all works on PHYSIOLOGY, HYDROPATHY, PHRENOLOGY, and the Natural Sciences generally. Booksellers supplied on the most liberal terms. AGENTS wanted in every State, county, and town. These works are universally popular, and thousands might be sold where they have never yet been introduced. Letters and other communications should, in ALL CASES, be post paid, and directed to the Publishers, as follows: FOWLER AND WELLS, 308 Broadway, N. Y.

Miscellaneous.

HOW TO WRITE: a New Pocket Manual

of Composition and Letter-Writing, embracing Hints on Penmanship and choice of Writing Materials, Practical Rules for Literary Composition in general, and Epistolary and Newspaper Writing, Punctuation, and Proof Correcting in particular; Directions for Writing Letters of Business, Relationship, Friendship and Love, Illustrated with numerous Examples of Genuine Epistles from the pens of the Best Writers, to which are added Forms for Letters of Introduction, Notes, Cards, &c. Paper, 30 cents; muslin, 50 cents.

HOW TO TALK: a New Pocket Manual

of Conversation and Debate, with Directions for Acquiring a Grammatical and Graceful Style, embracing the Origin of Language, a Condensed History of the English Language, a Practical Exposition of the Parts of Speech, and their Modifications and Arrangement in Sentences; Hints on Pronunciation, the Art of Conversation, Debating, Reading and Books, with more than Five Hundred Errors in Speaking Corrected. Paper, 30 cents; muslin, 50 cents.

HOW TO BEHAVE: a New Pocket Manual

of Republican Etiquette, and Guide to Correct Personal Habits; embracing an Exposition of the Principles of Good Manners, Useful Hints on the Care of the Person, Eating, Drinking, Exercise, Habits, Dress, Self-Culture, and Behavior at Home; the Etiquette of Salutations, Introductions, Receptions, Visits, Dinners, Evening Parties, Conversation, Letters, Presents, Weddings, Funerals, the Street, the Church, Places of Amusement, Traveling, &c; with Illustrative Anecdotes, a Chapter on Love and Courtship, and Rules of Order for Debating Societies. Paper, 30 cents; muslin, 50 cents.

HOW TO DO BUSINESS: a New Pocket

Manual of Practical Affairs and Guide to Success in Life; embracing the Principle, of Business; Advice in Reference to a Business Education; Choice of a Pursuit, Buying and Selling, General Management, Manufacturing, Mechanical Trades, Farming, Book and Newspaper Publishing, Miscellaneous Enterprises, Causes of Success and Failure, How to Get Customers, Business Maxims, Letter to a Young Lawyer, Business Forms, Legal and Useful Information, and a Dictionary of Commercial Terms. Paper, 30 cents; muslin, 50 cents.

HAND BOOKS FOR HOME IMPROVE-

MENT (Educational); comprising, "How to Write," "How to Talk," "How to Behave," and "How to Do Business," in one large gilt volume. Price, $1 50.

HOPES AND HELPS FOR THE YOUNG

of both Sexes; Relating to the Formation of Character, Choice of Avocati[illegible], Health, Amusement, Music, Conversation, Cultivation of Intellect, Moral S[illegible]ments, Social Affection, Courtship and Marriage. By Rev. G. S. Weaver. [illegible], in paper, 62 cents; muslin, 87 cents.

HINTS TOWARDS REFORMS; consisting of Lectures, Essays, Addresses, and other Writings. With the Crystal Palace and its Lessons. Second Edition, Enlarged. By Horace Greeley. Price, $1 25.

HUMAN RIGHTS, AND THEIR POLITI-cal guarantees. By Hurlbut. With Notes, by Combe. Paper, 62 cts.; muslin, 87 cts.

NATURAL LAWS OF MAN. A Philo-sophical Catechism. By J. G. Spurzheim, M. D. An important work. 30 cents.

HOME FOR ALL. A New, Cheap, Con-venient and Superior Mode of Building; containing Full Directions for Constructing Gravel Walls. With Views, Plans and Engraved Illustrations. Price, 87 cents.

DEMANDS OF THE AGE ON COLLEGES. A Speech Delivered by Hon. Horace Mann, President of Antioch College. With an Address to the Students on College Honor. Price, 25 cents.

AIMS AND AIDS FOR GIRLS AND YOUNG WOMEN, on the various duties of life, including Physical, Intellectual, and Moral Development; Self-Culture Improvement, Education, the Home Relations, their Duties to Young Men, Marriage, Womanhood, and Happiness. By Rev. G. S. Weaver. Paper, 62 cts.; muslin, 87 cts.

SCIENCE OF SWIMMING. Giving a History of Swimming, and Instructions to Learners. By an Experienced Swimmer. Illustrated with Engravings. 15 cents. Every boy should have a copy.

WAYS OF LIFE: or, the Right Way AND THE WRONG WAY. A First Rate Book for all Young People. By Rev. G. S. Weaver. Paper, 50 cts.; muslin, 60 cts.

DELIA'S DOCTORS: or, a Glance Behind the Scenes. By Hannah Gardner Creamer. Paper, price 62 cents; muslin 87 cents.

IMMORTALITY TRIUMPHANT. The Ex-istence of a God and Human Immortality, Practically Considered, and the Truth of Divine Revelation Substantiated. By Rev. John Bovee Dods. Muslin, 87 cts.

KANZAS REGION: Embracing Descrip-tions of Scenery, Climate, Productions, Soil, and Resources of the Territory. Interspersed with Incidents of Travel. By Max Greene. Price 30 cts; mus. 50 cts.

CHEMISTRY, AND ITS APPLICATIONS to Agriculture and Commerce. By Justus Liebig, M. D., F. R. S. Price 25 cents.

BOTANY FOR ALL CLASSES. Containing a Floral Dictionary, and a Glossary of Scientific Terms. Illustrated. 87 cents.

POPULATION, THEORY OF. Deduced from the General Law of Animal Fertility. Introduction by Dr. Trall. 15 cents.

LIFE ILLUSTRATED: A First-Class PICTORIAL WEEKLY FAMILY PAPER. Devoted to Entertainment, Improvement, and Progress To illustrate Life in all its phases, to point out all legitimate means of Economy and Profit, and to encourage a spirit of Hope, Activity, Self-Reliance, and Manliness among the People are some of the objects of this Journal. Published Weekly, at $2 a year. Half a year, $1.

TOBACCO. Three Prize Essays. By Drs. Shew, Trall, and Baldwin. Price, 15 cents.——TOBACCO: its History, Nature, and Effects on Body and Mind. 30 cents.——USE OF TOBACCO; its Physical, Intellectual, and Moral Effects. By Dr. Alcott. 15 cents.——SOBER AND TEMPERATE LIFE; the Discourses and Letters of Louis Cornaro. With a Biography of the Author. With Notes and an Appendix. 30 cents. Twenty-five thousand copies have been sold. It is translated into several languages.——TEA AND COFFEE; their Physical, Intellectual, and Moral Effects on the Human System. By Dr. W. Alcott. 15 cents.——TEETH; their Structure, Disease and Treatment. With numerous Illustrations. By John Burdell. Price, 15 cts.

Mesmerism and Psychology.

A NEW AND COMPLETE LIBRARY OF MESMERISM AND PSCYHOLOGY, embracing the most popular works on the subject, with suitable Illustrations. In two volumes of about 900 pp. Price, $3 00.

ELECTRICAL PSYCHOLOGY, Physiology of. In a Course of Twelve Lectures. By John Bovee Dods. Muslin. Price, 87 cents.

MACROCOSM AND MICROCOSM; or, the Universe Without and the Universe Within; in the World of Sense, and the World of Soul. By Wm. Fishbough. Price, Paper, 62 cents; Muslin, 87 cents.

FASCINATION; or. the Philosophy of Charming. Illustrating the Principles of Life, in connection with Spirit and Matter. By J. B. Newman, M. D. 87 cents.

PHILOSOPHY OF MESMERISM. Six Lectures. With an Introduction. By Rev. John Bovee Dods. Paper. Price, 30 cents.

PSYCHOLOGY; or, the Science of the Soul. Considered Physiologically and Philosophically. With an Appendix containing Notes of Mesmeric and Psychical Experience. By Joseph Haddock, M.D. 30 cts.

THESE works may be ordered in large or small quantities. A liberal discount will be made to AGENTS, and others, who buy to sell again. They may be sent by Express, or as Freight, by Railroad, Steamships, Sailing Vessels, by Stage, or Canal, to any City, Town, or Village, in the United States, the Canadas, to Europe, or any place on the Globe. Checks or drafts, for large amounts, on New York, Philadelphia, or Boston, always preferred. We pay cost of exchange. All letters should be post paid, and addressed as follows:

BOSTON: 142 W[illegible]ington St. — **FOWLER AND WELLS, 308 Broadway, New York.** — PHILADELPHIA: 922 Chestnut St.

www.ingramcontent.com/pod-product-compliance
Lightning Source LLC
LaVergne TN
LVHW010154110826
845151LV00002B/511

* 9 7 8 1 4 2 5 5 3 7 2 1 0 *